ROOTS of HEALING

Quotes About Michael Toms

"...one of the best interviewers who has ever worked the American airwaves, radio or TV."

— Robert Fuller, physicist, educator, past president of Oberlin College, and active citizen diplomat

"Someone with whom I have cruised some important realms of the cosmic ocean and in doing so have developed ever increasing confidence in his intuitive navigation."

— R. Buckminster Fuller (1895-1983), inventor of the geodesic dome; designer, philosopher, and creator of the World Games

"...Bill Moyers and Michael Toms are alike: two of the most creative interviewers it has been my good fortune to work with."

— Joseph Campbell (1904-1987), mythologist and author of *Hero with a Thousand Faces, The Masks of God, Myths to Live By,* and *The Mythic Image*

◈ ◈ ◈

ROOTS of HEALING

THE NEW MEDICINE

◈ ◈ ◈

Andrew Weil, M.D.,
and other contributors

With Michael Toms

Hay House, Inc.
Carlsbad, CA

Published and distributed in the United States by:
Hay House, Inc., P.O. Box 5100, Carlsbad, CA 92018-5100
(800) 654-5126 • (800) 650-5115 (fax)

Edited by: Jill Kramer • Designed by: Jenny Richards

The authors of this book do not dispense medical advice or prescribe the use of any technique as a form of treatment for physical or medical problems without the advice of a physician, either directly or indirectly. The intent of the authors is only to offer information of a general nature to help you in your quest for emotional well-being and good health. In the event you use any of the information in this book for yourself, which is your constitutional right, the authors and the publisher assume no responsibility for your actions.

Library of Congress Cataloging-in-Publication Data

Roots of healing : the new medicine / Andrew Weil, and other contributors, with Michael Toms.
p. cm.
Includes bibliographical references.
ISBN 1-56170-422-9 (trade paper)
1. Alternative medicine. 2. Medicine—Philosophy. 3. Mind and body therapies. 4. Physician and patient. I. Toms, Michael.
R733.W444 1997
615.5—dc21 96-49306
CIP

ISBN 1-56170-422-9

00 99 98 97 5 4 3 2
First Printing, March 1997
Second Printing, April 1997

Printed in the United States of America

Contents

PART II: PSYCHOSPIRITUAL APPROACHES

PART III: CHANGING PERCEPTIONS OF COMPLEMENTARY THERAPY

Dedicated to the memory of Rev. Barbara St. Andrews,
whose life was about healing.

PREFACE

ABOUT NEW DIMENSIONS

New Dimensions Radio is the major activity of the New Dimensions Foundation, a nonprofit educational organization. "New Dimensions" is a national public radio interview series featuring thousands of hours of in-depth discussions on a wide variety of topics. **Michael Toms,** the co-founder of New Dimensions Radio, award-winning host of the "New Dimensions" interview series—and a widely respected New Paradigm spokesperson and scholar himself—engages in thoughtful, intimate dialogues with the leading thinkers and social innovators of our time focusing on positive approaches to the challenges of a changing society.

◈ ◈ ◈

ABOUT THIS BOOK

Roots of Healing comprises in-depth discussions between Michael Toms; Andrew Weil, M.D., the best-selling author of *Spontaneous Healing;* and more than 20 other health-care professionals who explore the changing face of healing in the West. Some of the issues discussed include the future possibilities offered by complementary medicine, what to do when faced with ethical choices in medical care, how you as a patient can take more responsibility for your care, the medicinal value of foods and herbs, how Chinese and Ayurvedic medicines approach health and healing, how to recognize your own inner healing potential, the relevance of the mind/body connection, the sociopolitical considerations in our changing health-care system, and more.

◈◈◈◈◈

(The original *Roots of Healing* public radio series from which the book was compiled was produced with the support of the Fetzer Institute.)

Introduction by Michael Toms

Health care in America is changing. It has to. We spend more money on health care here than any other developed nation, and yet the system is a shambles. Americans are less satisfied with their health-care system than anywhere else in the developed world. Millions have little or no health coverage. Millions more live in fear that their insurance will be canceled because their insurer may suddenly find them ineligible. One in five Americans are locked into a job because they can't be sure they can get adequate health-care benefits elsewhere.

A recent *USA Today* study showed that in the United States, patients made more visits to complementary care-givers than to family doctors and internists. This fact vividly demonstrates that people are seeking new ways to address their health and are open to complementary approaches. At the same time, the National Institute of Health (NIH) has created the Office of Alternative Medicine to begin researching some of the newly emerging techniques and methodologies in this rapidly growing new field of medicine.

And yet for all the discussion about health-care reforms we read and hear about today, the focus is almost solely on the how to pay for the health-care system and how to give more people access to it. Notable goals, to be sure, but the deeper issue points to the redefinition of health and healing. We need to look beyond the mere absence of disease as the definition for health, to reexamine the patient-doctor contract, look closely at the individual's responsibility for health, review our contemporary emphasis on acute care, and determine what's possible through preventive medicine and complementary approaches.

ROOTS OF HEALING: The New Medicine is about opening the dialogue to explore some of these issues. This book will raise more questions than it provides answers to, but this is where the healing process begins—being open to possibilities. Mind/body medicine is not a cure-all, any more than nutrition and exercise promise miracle solutions to illness. And yet the recognition of how our attitudes, perceptions, and thoughts are connected to the body's capacity for healing can lead to real value for those who are ill and well alike.

◈◈◈◈◈

PART I

The Healers and the Healed

CHAPTER ONE

The Changing Dynamics in the Doctor/Patient Relationship

Contributors:

Helene S. Smith, Ph.D., is a microbiologist and cancer researcher affiliated with both the California Pacific Medical Center and the University of California. Best known for her work on the response of breast cancer to chemotherapy, she appeared in a cancer feature in *Natural Health* magazine.

Andrew Weil, M.D., received his training at Harvard Medical School and is the Associate Director of Medicine at the University of Arizona. He is the author of

Spontaneous Healing; Health and Healing: Understanding Conventional and Alternative Medicine; and *Natural Medicine: A Comprehensive Manual for Wellness and Self-Care.*

Daniel Goleman, Ph.D., is the author of *Emotional Intelligence; Vital Lies, Simple Truths; The Meditative Mind;* and is the editor of *Mind/ Body Medicine: How to Use Your Mind for Better Health.*

◈ ◈ ◈

MICHAEL TOMS: *Let's begin by asking you to tell us how you see the mind/body connection, how it's affecting the patient-doctor relationship, how the emergence of what we'll call "the new medicine" is having an impact on what the healer does with the healed, and how the healed relates to the healer.*

ANDREW WEIL: If we admit a mind/body connection, and if we admit that we can accelerate healing processes or activate healing mechanisms through interventions at the mental level, then the impact of a doctor's belief system and a doctor's words on a patient become very important. Physicians now are not trained in how to use words, in how to use the projection of belief onto them from patients. In many cases, they use that projected belief very negatively and destructively.

I have collected many cases of what I call "medical hexing" or "medical cursing." I think that most of this is done completely unconsciously; it's not done maliciously.

But in one way or another, doctors say things to patients that suggest that healing is not possible, that diseases cannot be cured, that patients will have to live with conditions forever, that there's no hope. I'm interested in where that pessimism comes from in medicine, why doctors don't believe in healing. I'm interested in the fact that doctors are so poorly trained in how to use words correctly. I think that if doctors are very sensitive to the kind of projection of belief, to the power of words, to the power of the belief system of both doctor and patient to effect healing mechanisms in the body, that makes the doctor-patient interaction supremely important, you know, possibly even more important than the specifics of treatments that are prescribed.

HELENE S. SMITH: I think that the whole perspective of a physician in the past, both from his or her training and from the perspective of how our society views the physician, is that it's a vertical system, with the physician telling the patient what to do and knowing the answers for the patient. And as many of us know, no one knows the answers for anyone else. The assumption that the physician does know creates a different perspective, and I think that's the root of the problem. As I see it, a physician needs to change his or her perspective from being the chief in a vertical system to a partner with the patient. And the patient needs to change the perspective from looking for a surrogate parent who explains how to fix the body, just like a mechanic will tell you how to fix your car, to acknowledging responsibility for having to take charge of the body him- or herself.

***MICHAEL:** Helene, you are a molecular biologist who has been part of the achievement of Western medicine to reach this pinnacle of being able to use technology to provide curing for people. At the same time, when you yourself were faced with your own breast cancer, you opted to do something different from the traditional route that we're used to. I'm wondering how that happened for you.*

HELENE: Well, my perspective of a physician is very different, because in this vertical paradigm, the doctor talks to the patient, but the scientist talks to the doctor. And the basis in our medical schools is that the reason the doctor knows the answer for the patient is because science tells the doctor. Now, because I was a scientist, I knew that what science tells the doctor isn't always right, and so it was easier for me to understand that a doctor doesn't know the answers because I, as a scientist doing research in breast cancer, knew that I didn't know the answers. The relationship between me and a physician was a very different one. A physician might call me to ask me what to do, and so I'm at both ends of the spectrum—namely, telling the doctor what to do and then having the doctor tell me what to do. Because of that peculiar situation, I could easily see that the paradigm wasn't going to work. So for me, it was very simple to recognize that the doctor didn't know anything. I knew that all along because I knew the data, and so the doctor would say, "Well, there's such-and-such study that says you should do this," and I could tell that doctor why that study was flawed. That's a very unusual perspective, and one we certainly can't expect every patient to have.

MICHAEL: *How did the doctor respond to this situation, in your case?*

HELENE: Well, that was very interesting. Sometimes some of the doctors were friends of mine, and to some extent it was very difficult for them, because, for at least some of my physicians, I was their boss for research. I'm sure that, from a personal level, it was very hard for them to have to deal with me as a patient. They did it very beautifully, and we were able to talk about it. But these were people who were very close to me professionally. Some of the other doctors couldn't deal with it at all, and so I went to doctors and then just didn't go back. Others I knew I couldn't go to because they were too close to me professionally, and I didn't think either of us could handle it.

Some doctors accepted what I wanted and needed and were very helpful, and understood that, in the end, no matter what they did with other patients, they had to treat me differently. Those doctors, I suspect, do the same thing for every patient—namely, size up the patient, get a sense of what that patient needs, and then become that patient's servant, in the sense of serving the needs of the patient. That probably defines physicians, no matter who they are and what the needs of the patients are. And there may be patients who need an absolute authoritative answer, even though it may be wrong.

MICHAEL: *Do you have any insights to share with other patients who may find themselves in a similar situation, being diagnosed with an illness? What do they do?*

HELENE: Well, I sometimes say that some questions are too important to answer rationally, and in the end you collect all the information you can, and then you have to trust your inner voice. I don't know how other people do it. I only know how I do it, and there are many tools. I use meditation a lot. I've used psychic cards; I've just waited for an answer to come. In the end, I just know. And then, after I think I know, I get scared, and I say, "You don't really know!" And then I say, "Maybe I was wrong!" And then I run a whole lot of tapes, and then I go back to a place where I say, "I know." And then, that's what I have to do. Maybe I'm wrong, but that's also part of living, to accept responsibility for making a choice and doing it.

ANDREW: I'd like to comment on the "vertical relationship" that Helene referred to between doctors and patients. I do a lot of work in Japan; I go there frequently and lecture to doctors and medical schools and give seminars for Japanese doctors on moving in a holistic direction. I would say they're about ten years behind us in the new medical movement over there. Japanese medicine is much more authoritarian than American medicine, and you can see many of the faults of our system magnified where they're obvious and very visible. For example, Japanese patients never ask questions of doctors. It's not done. And a doctor is very offended if a patient asks a question. Japanese cancer patients are still never told that they have cancer. This is always justified as being in the best interest of the patient, but in fact it maintains a real imbalance of power between the doctor and the patient.

Typically, Japanese doctors, many of them, now see 30 patients an hour. They're called "two-minute doctors." Often they'll see the patient very quickly and issue a prescription. So this is really the ultimate vertical relationship between a doctor and a patient. There are many aspects of that still present in American medicine. They are changing. When I was growing up, I remember my family doctor would give prescriptions written in Latin that were unintelligible, and you would go to a drugstore and hand them over a high counter that was designed to prevent you from seeing what went on behind there. And the pharmacist would give you a bottle of pills, and you never asked what they were or what they did. Now that seems unthinkable today. So things are moving in a better direction. Still, there's a long way to go.

And yet, part of me feels that it would not be totally in everyone's best interest to deconstruct this verticality totally, because, as I mentioned, there is a real art to medical practice. I think, essentially, that the practice of medicine is an art, not a science. I think it can use the forms of science and information provided by science, but ultimately, the manner in which a doctor deals with a patient is an art. And the art of medicine, I think, is the intuitive selection and presentation of treatments to patients in ways that maximally impact with their belief system in the service of healing. And that uses some of the power that patients project onto doctors. I don't want to see that go away totally. I think that the doctor can work as the patient's servant, can work in partnership with a patient. But still, there's the aspect of a projected belief onto doctors that can be used very creatively to increase the probability of healing.

HELENE: Aren't you really saying that you think doctors are shamans?

ANDREW: Yes.

HELENE: Then, if you think about, in all other religious traditions, how a shaman is trained, how do you see the way doctors need to be trained?

ANDREW: Much differently from the way that they're now being trained. First of all, shamans have learned through their own experience of states of illness, of states of disordered consciousness. Many medical students have no such experience. I thought the recent movie *The Doctor* was excellent with William Hurt. You know, it really showed the evolution of a doctor as a result of going through the experience of being a patient with cancer. I think students need to have more real experience. They also need to learn how to make themselves models of healthy living, because I think one of the most effective ways that doctors can teach is by themselves being good examples. And the process of medical education now, in a way, encourages very unhealthy lifestyles and habits. I mean, how can a medical student possibly take time to meditate, for example, or even, let alone, to have good exercise habits or good nutrition habits? So I think that there is a great need for a radical change in medical education—not simply juggling curriculums around, and every few years there's curriculum reform—but it seems to me it's a shuffling of things around. There's no real change. Real change would involve giving students the opportunity to have more direct experience, to learn from nature, to learn to develop good health habits themselves.

HELENE: Well, what I think you're saying is that you wouldn't deconstruct the role of the doctor; you would deconstruct the role of the medical school.

ANDREW: Yes.

HELENE: And my eyes roll back to the top of my head when I think of the practicality of having to do that.

ANDREW: I tried for a number of years to get one lecture in the medical curriculum at the University of Arizona on smoking as an addiction. I can't think of anything more important. Here's the number-one preventable cause of serious illness, and there was no lecture on the subject of smoking as an addiction and what to do about it. It took me about five years to get anyone to make space in the curriculum for such a thing. So my eyes roll back, also.

MICHAEL: It reminds me of reading this statistic in the preparation of this program that one out of five Americans dies of a smoking-related disease. One out of five—twenty percent! That's incredible.

HELENE: I wanted to get back to this concept that the only place to really change the practice of medicine is to change the practice of medical schools. I believe that the only way to change the practice of medical schools may be to change the whole society and the consumers' demand, and the way medical schools respond to money. Money comes from the federal government in the form of grants. It comes from the consumers who go to the hospitals of the medical school. There has to be a whole paradigm shift in our society in order to get the institutions of medicine to respond.

DANIEL GOLEMAN: It's the original low-tech technology. All you need is a mind, and you can do it. So I think from that point of view, it represents a direct threat to the tendency to have high-tech, high-cost medicine. However, the real revolution is not in economics, because probably these services are somewhat profitable for hospitals. They wouldn't have them if they weren't. The real change is in the thinking of physicians, because when virtually all of the physicians who were practicing today went to medical school, the science they learned told them that there was no relationship between the immune system and the central nervous system, the brain, and therefore they always saw people's internal states, their feelings about what was happening to them about their illness as irrelevant to healing them. It's really a radical paradigm shift that's required for physicians to even grant that there might be a connection, because everything they've learned about biology, about the body, about disease, left that off the map.

This is really patient-centered care. This is care that

looks at the whole person, not just the disease. There have been rising levels of dissatisfaction among medical consumers about being treated like cogs in a medical machine. This fits right in, because it says, "Hey, you have to pay attention to me as a person. You have to attend to my internal feelings about what's going on, as well as give me good medical care, because if you don't, it will undermine your medical care."

Let me tell you about a really amazing study about doctor-patient relationships. They talked to people in waiting rooms of physicians' offices, and they asked, "How many questions do you have for your physician?" And on average, people had about four things they really wanted to know. Then, when people came out, they said, "Well, how many were you able to ask?" And on average, it was 1.6. Then they started watching patient-physician interactions, and they found out that within the first 18 seconds of a patient speaking, the doctor would cut him off and direct the conversation elsewhere, and never get back to where they had started. They're realizing that this was completely undermining, not completely, but largely, undermining what the physician was trying to do. For years in medicine they've been struggling with the fact that there are very low compliance rates. A doctor will give a pill or a regimen to a patient and say, "Now, I want you to do this." They'd find that huge percentages, 50 percent or more sometimes, would not do what the physicians said. And it was because the physician hadn't really communicated with the patient.

ANDREW: Well, certainly this raises the issue of communication, which is what we've been talking about, and

I think this is an area in which physicians are poorly trained. And again it comes back to how can we do it differently. How can we produce a new breed of doctors who have a different paradigm, who have different skills? I think what Helene said earlier, that these are really market-driven or economy-driven phenomena, is very important. At the moment, there is a large consumers' movement building in this society that's demanding different services and different kinds of treatment from doctors. I think that's our best hope. You know, these changes are not originating within the medical profession, and certainly not within medical schools. It's that patients are demanding that doctors treat them differently. And if medical doctors don't do it, they'll go elsewhere. That's putting great pressure on the medical profession to respond.

HELENE: I couldn't agree more. I think the only hope of changing the system is through the consumer. I may be a bit more pessimistic than Andrew. Perhaps it won't be that the doctor takes a new role, even though that might be most desirable. Perhaps the doctor will take a side role, namely the technologist. The doctor will be the technologist, the nuts-and-bolts person, and there will emerge a patient advocate, perhaps a nurse practitioner, someone who gets elevated to the role of shaman or healer. That will happen because the consumer accepts it. If the consumer accepts a different paradigm, and it flourishes, then the institutions will create it because that's what the consumer will pay for.

◈ ◈ ◈

SUMMARY

How doctors talk with patients is extremely important to the healing process. Many patients expect their doctors to have all the answers, and many doctors do their best to fulfill that role. This may lead, however, to patient frustration, doctor burnout, and incomplete healing. With the best of intentions, doctors have even said things to their patients that have led patients to give up hope and die sooner than expected. This is known as psychological malpractice, or "doctor hexing." This awareness is leading doctors to reexamine what they tell their patients. They are beginning to understand how important good communication is to successful treatment. New expectations for a doctor/patient collaboration are fueling changes. Patients are taking more responsibility for their treatments, and doctors are learning that their patients' psychological and spiritual condition is just as important as their physical health in the course of illness.

CHAPTER TWO

PATIENT-CENTERED CARE—CREATING A NEW PARADIGM IN MIND/BODY MEDICINE

Contributors:

Duane Walker, R.N., M.S., F.A.A.N., is Director of the Queen's Medical Center in Honolulu, Hawaii, a highly respected private hospital that places a strong emphasis on holistic care. (Health-care statistics in Hawaii are among the most favorable in the nation.)

Tracey Cosgrove, M.L.I.S., is the Director of the Planetree Resource Center, a consumer health library at the innovative California Pacific Medical Center, whose vision of health care extends to human caring, family involvement, and consumer education.

Helene S. Smith, Ph.D., and **Andrew Weil, M.D.** (see bios on page 1)

◈ ◈ ◈

MICHAEL TOMS: *A tangible example of the ideas expressed in the previous chapter is the Queen's Medical Center in Honolulu. [I spoke with Duane Walker and asked him to talk about the wing of the hospital that is devoted to total patient care.]*

DUANE WALKER: We have one wing of the hospital that is all private rooms. It's two nursing units, a total of 48 beds. The project started out as a care redesign, and we finally came up with a name called *Lokomaikai* [sic], which is a Hawaiian word that stands for inner health, inner strength, and peace. On this particular unit, what we're attempting to do is to be patient-centered and take things to the patient, involve the patient in the care, empower the patient. Some of the techniques that we build into that is just a total assessment at the time the patient is admitted, and to explain to them our philosophy, that we want them to participate in the decisions.

Along with that, because we're very much a transcultural community, or state, we really have started looking at different aspects of the cultures of the patients who are admitted here, and have embarked on a very vigorous educational program with our staff, because we feel they need to have a better understanding. We've had programs on tai chi, meditation, relaxation, therapeutic touch, acupuncture, herbal therapy, and so on. And what we've found with our staff is that that's become part of their own lives, that they're able to share that with the patients. The other thing that I think is a big change for a hospital is that we don't have any visiting hours. They're totally open on that unit, 24 hours a day. If loved ones want to stay overnight, we encourage them to participate in the care. With many of our ethnic-group patients, we encourage them to bring in their own food that they're used to, and then what we do is work with them as to how that either enhances or needs to be changed with whatever type of medical problem they have. We have a library on the unit that we've set up, and the greatest feature about it is that it's hooked into the computer to our library here on our campus, so if a person is a new diabetic, the staff can do a Medline search for them, or we try to help the patient actually do the Medline search. And then the library faxes over copies of the article.

We'll be coming out with initiatives soon saying that the total hospital is going to move in that direction, not just that one unit. The successes that we're having in that program—we intend on taking parts of it and moving that philosophy to other wings of the hospital. There's very, very good support coming from both the board and from our medical staff.

We're looking at some of the things we're doing there involving the patient that really do help us reduce costs, and we think that we're further ahead. I think that by working with our patients from an educational viewpoint, we're decreasing the length of stay, and decreasing the readmission rates for chronic patients.

MICHAEL: *The differences that you mentioned in Hawaii, relative to the population and the openness to other aspects of healing...I'm wondering: Has this been incorporated into the medical training program there at the university?*

DUANE: That's the ironic part, because we didn't start out that way, but now the residency program in internal medicine is located primarily on that floor, with the objective being that future doctors need to move in that direction. It was just kind of a fluke, and it's been the most wonderful thing that's happened to us.

MICHAEL: *Tracey, as Planetree spreads out and influences other hospitals, is it like a franchise operation, or how does it actually work? What are the requirements for other hospitals to actually call themselves "Planetree"?*

TRACEY: I think it's best to think of it more as a consortium of folks who get together. When I say "folks," I mean people in health care who want their institutions to really become more humanized in their health-care delivery and to follow certain aspect of Planetree concepts. And when I say that, I mean that patients should be able to have access to information, that there's an arts program that's part of the hospital experience. It might include storytelling and music. If patients choose, they can follow a self-medication program so that they can participate in taking their own medications and aren't always beholden to hospital staff for that. Also, the family can be more involved.

We have what's called a "care partner program," where family members can learn to do more of the care of their loved ones themselves. And among all the different things that make up a Planetree approach to health care, there are medical centers and hospitals and a growing number of other kinds of institutions, like skilled nursing facilities, that are wanting to ascribe to these principles and be able to say that they really want their health care to be delivered in this fashion.

What's been really interesting is that it's not a franchise or cookie-cutter approach. It's people taking these principles and then going with their own interpretation of it. While there might be arts programs at different medical centers, they're doing different things. And it's the most inspiring thing to see what somebody's interpretation of music could be, or art could be, for people on the hospital unit.

MICHAEL: *Tracey, how did you personally get involved in the Planetree Resource Center?*

TRACEY: I have to say that what attracted me to Planetree was my own experiences of the hospital patient. Many years ago, I had a very rare disorder and went in the hospital. It was a pediatric condition. Even though I was an adult, it was very difficult to diagnose because I wasn't the average kind of person to get this diagnosis. It was the people in my life who did the research and found the articles who talked about how specialists were treating this in other parts of the United States. I'm from Portland,

Oregon, and there weren't a lot of these cases there at the time. My physicians contacted those specialists, found out how to treat this condition, and in effect, ending up saving my life. I discovered early on in my adult life how important information is, and what the power of it can be in helping keep people well and treat illness. When I moved to San Francisco, I was only here a week when I discovered Planetree, when I was just walking down the street.

MICHAEL: *So you provide information about all of the approaches to health that are out there?*

TRACEY: Our response is if people come in and ask for information on a particular subject or a particular healing practice, we'll do our best to try to find that information by using databases and the resources we already have on-site. We really don't feel like we're in the position to tell people what they should be learning about their health and what they should read and not read and what will work and not work. We really think that it is up to the individual to make an informed decision based on resources and information that are available, and our goal is to give people access to those resources.

In many cases, we may have already gathered together materials on that specific diagnosis. One of the things that you'd find in the library is files of articles that we've gathered from medical journals, holistic health publications, consumer health newsletters and magazines, pamphlets if they're unbiased in presentation and not sponsored by drug companies, or something like that.

Almost half of the people who are coming in are those who don't have a specific medical problem themselves, but have family members or a good friend who is sick. They want to know what's going on, and information for them can be very reassuring. Maybe it's not about making a personal medical decision for them, but it's about understanding what's going on for their friend or loved one, and learning how to be a support person for the patient.

HELENE S. SMITH: Well, being at California Pacific Medical Center myself, I have seen some of the most remarkable accomplishments of the Planetree program. I have to say that I think it's totally a direction that I would like to see medicine go in. The program in Hawaii sounds absolutely marvelous. I also see some of the difficulties of moving that program into the mainstream of the hospital, and I wonder, when Duane Walker says it's going to take five years, my thought is I hope it *only* takes five years. I would like to see it happen tomorrow. Most likely it will be somewhere between the 10 or 15 years that I think it will actually take, and the tomorrow when I'd like to see it happen. We need to analyze the impediments. I think we get back to the place where Andrew and I started talking about this, the doctor's perception. Some of the doctors are very excited about the Planetree program, and what I find very exciting about California Pacific Medical Center is that I do find clinician colleagues who are excited about it. But many of them are not. They find it very threatening and very difficult to deal with this new paradigm of approaching their patient. And I wonder how as a society we can focus and martial our resources to make that happen more effectively and more efficiently and sooner.

ANDREW WEIL: Well, I'm delighted to hear about all experiments of this kind. I think it's great. At the same time, I have to tell you that I think that conventional hospitals are doomed as institutions. I think that they're going to become more and more economically unworkable. I would foresee a time when each region might have one conventional hospital where high-tech conventional medicine is practiced, and that's where you go for MRI scans and high-tech surgery, and so forth. And I would like to see the appearance of a wholly new kind of institution that would be something between a hospital and a spa. I don't know what we'd call them, maybe "health and healing centers," where people could go, and when they came out they would know more than they went in with about how to eat, about how to exercise, about how to handle stress, where there are a variety of healing techniques offered by a variety of health-care practitioners. This would be reimbursed by the insurance.

I think that if we look at the total spectrum of illness, that which requires the interventions of conventional medicine is a distinct minority, maybe 10 to 20 percent of all cases of illness. And most of the other things—arthritis, allergies, many autoimmune conditions, all chronic degenerative disease—these could be better dealt with in these new kinds of institutions that came from a different model and different paradigm to begin with.

◈ ◈ ◈

SUMMARY

Hospitals such as the Queens Medical Center in Hawaii and the Planetree unit at California Pacific Medical Center have shown that patient-centered care can enhance healing and even have economic benefits. These programs allow patients to see and make notes in their own charts, to have visitors when they want, and to take responsibility for their own medication. They also teach family members how to participate in care. The Planetree Patient Resource Library and others like it are available by telephone to people from any part of the country who wish to research the most up-to-date information on their own, or a loved one's, illness.

◈◈◈◈◈

CHAPTER THREE

Questions of Ethics

Contributors:

Daniel Dugan, Ph.D., is the Director of the Health Care Ethics Consulting Service at The Park Ridge Center for the Study of Health, Faith, and Ethics in Chicago.

Larry Greenfield, R.N., M.S., F.A.A.N., is Vice-President, Coordinator of Research, and Resident Scholar in Theology and Ministry for The Park Ridge Center.

Robert Moss, M.D., was (at the time of this interview) the Co-Director of the Program for Clinical Ethics and Medical Humanities at the Park Ridge Center. He is currently the Co-Director of Geriatric Medicine at Lutheran General Hospital, Park Ridge, Illinois; and is also a

Clinical Associate Professor of Medicine at the University of Chicago.

Helene S. Smith, Ph.D., and **Andrew Weil, M.D.** (see bios on page 1)

◈ ◈ ◈

MICHAEL TOMS: *[One of the organizations we visited in the preparation of this book was the Park Ridge Center for the Study of Health, Faith, and Ethics in Chicago. This organization collaborates with representatives from diverse cultures, religious communities, health-care fields, and academic disciplines, and disseminates its findings to people interested in health, religion, and ethics. What they're trying to do is to bring the spirit of healing, or the healing spirit, into the process of health care and healing. We interviewed Daniel Dugan, Robert Moss, and Larry Greenfield.]*

DANIEL DUGAN: The new thing about ethics in our time really comes from the explosion of new technologies, the pressure of economics, and the pressure of the law. It has put choices into the hands of people that they have never had before. When I was a child, my great-grand-mother, Mary, who was 93, slowly got sick. She was upstairs in her bed, and all of us went in and out and took care of her. When she stopped eating and drinking, we mopped her brow and kept her lips moist, but there was no big decision about whether to put tubes in her or to hook her up to machines or whatever.

Now, medical technology does put the wherewithal to prolong biological processes more or less indefinitely into human hands. Those decisions are not just technical medical decisions. They call for a sense of who this patient is, and the story that this person has been living, and what has made this person's life worth living. Therefore, the decisions about matters like this will have to be joint ventures. And what ethics is about theoretically is the study of values and motivations and the reflection on the long-term consequences of what we do. Clinical Ethics, my work, is how to help patients, families, doctors, nurses, pastors, rabbis, and others on a daily basis who are forced to make decisions about medical treatments in an atmosphere of high uncertainty. And when there may be disagreements, it's about how to help that process move to some kind of consensus so that everybody feels like "we did the best we could," where the decisions are least likely to be regretted.

In 1982, one percent of acute-care hospitals in the United States had organized ethics committees. By 1993, more than 60 percent had organized ethics committees, and between 25 and 30 percent of nursing homes have formed such committees. These are grass-roots committees, with an interest in helping decision-makers think through their decisions, and providing a forum to do that. It is growing and deepening, in the sense that it used to be focused just on the tough, dramatic, high-drama, single-moment-of-decision kinds of cases, or the ones where the machines were very, very prominent. As it emerges and matures as a field, Clinical Ethics in organizations is increasingly interested in looking more generally at patients' and families' experiences of how they are treated from the time they move into the building, of how the signs work to help them, to the quality of the way they are spoken to and assisted, right on through to the decision-making. So the idea is that ethics is being seen more as something that's meant to pervade the whole community.

ROBERT MOSS: Ethics for me has provided a way to work on the issue of what is the right thing to do for the patient, from the patient's perspective. I think physicians right now are overwhelmed by the complexities of medicine. They're faced with making some very difficult decisions with patients; trying to understand what it is the patient wants, trying to deal with the prognostic uncertainties of the conditions they have, trying to put those decisions within the context of a system of law and economic constraints being placed at the bedside in the care of patients. I think physicians and all health-care team members actually welcome the invocation of ethics into medicine.

Ultimately, I think the goal is to improve patient care by enhancing patient decision-making and the patient-physician relationship. We hope to develop a more holistic approach to the care of the patient, not just involving the patient, but other members of the health-care team, including social workers, nurses, and members from pastoral care. I think we're in an age where patient autonomy, respect for persons, and patient rights is probably the most important area in medicine. The traditional physician used to be more paternalistic. We used to enter the room and pronounce to the patient the best treatment alternative and the way things should be done. I think when we did that we were trying to act in the patient's best interest, but we really took the patient out of participating in decision-making.

LARRY GREENFIELD: The general approach here is when people are predisposed to say, "Ah! This is a problem we can solve in steps one-two-three," we say, "Now wait a minute! Now hold on! There's more going on here. There's a whole human being here." It's more than simply mind-body; there's mind-body-spirit; there's more than self here; there's self-family-culture. There's a whole continuum within the individual, that individual's family, the place of the family and individual in a neighborhood, a culture. Let's be sensitive to that. This is a person who defines herself or himself in terms of a set of values, a set of meanings, that may or may not be connected with a mainline religious tradition. So we're saying this not only to the clinician, but we're saying it to ourselves—because religious types, clergy types, can be fairly narrow and kind of set in their practices. We're saying to both communities, "Be aware of this more whole dimension, this more thoroughgoing, expansive reality that we call the individual." That probably is a misnomer itself. I mean that there isn't such a thing as an individual in any complete sense. There's always individual and community, just as all communities are made up of individuals.

ANDREW WEIL: One thing that struck me in Daniel Dugan's remarks was his reference to the atmosphere of high uncertainty. I know that Helene as a scientist certainly places great emphasis on certainty, but I'm struck by how little that concept has made it into medical thinking. We medical doctors still act as if there is certainty in the universe, that we can come to certain diagnoses. I think if you accept the fact that we live with uncertainty, that we live in a probabilistic universe, then what we want to do is learn how to be good gamblers. We want to know how to play odds. Doctors don't do that very well, and they don't instruct patients how to do it very well.

For example, I was looking over some reports of an insurance company here in the Bay Area that has done a lot of analysis of why health-care costs are what they are. I saw case after case in which an MRI scan had been ordered for headaches as the first line in investigation to find out why people were having headaches. Now, I, as a doctor, can analyze most cases of headache just by talking with people. You know, most cases of headaches are due to muscle tension. Some are due to vascular instability that can be traced to particular causes. The chance that a headache is due to some mass space-occupying lesion in the skull, which you can find with an MRI scan, is pretty low down on the probability scale. So that's not the thing you do first, if you're working with odds and learning how to play probabilities, and by not doing that, that's one reason why health-care costs are what they are, and the medical system is sinking.

HELENE S. SMITH: I think Andy's exactly right. People are very uncomfortable with probabilities. They want to know for themselves what the answer is, and they don't want to have to acknowledge that it's uncertain, that it may depend on how much of their own lives they change, and that after they do all of those things that for at least some illnesses that are acute, it's a matter of grace, and there is a mystery, and that some people have, quote, a "spontaneous remission" from the worst illnesses. It requires a great deal of letting go of all of what we think we are as Western people, and that's asking a lot of people when they suddenly get sick. Unless people have been thinking that way their whole lives, even if they *are* thinking that way their whole lives, getting sick is a very difficult time to do it. In fact, I've often said that preparing for dying is much too difficult to do when you're sick. These are the kinds of issues that are more than our medical system as it exists now can change. It can only come from below, from the consumer, and from our whole society changing.

The medical establishment actually is much better at changing than many other institutions. If you think about some other institutions, such as education or religion, how fast do our religious institutions change? Doctors, for all their getting a bum rap for being conservative, are actually on the forefront of changing quickly. How fast do our politicians change their styles? We are asking an enormous amount of a young physician. We're asking a young physician to become a wise old person, and to do it in four years of medical school. That's a lot.

ANDREW: Well, I'm thrilled to hear a scientist use the word *mystery*. I think that's terrific and, again, if medicine could regain its ancient ties with magic and religion, I think it would be much more comfortable to have doctors live with uncertainty and the idea that there is mystery and that sometimes we just don't know why some people get better and some people don't.

◈ ◈ ◈

SUMMARY

New technologies have given us new choices in the care of gravely ill people. This, in turn, creates many dilemmas: When is it appropriate to remove life support? Should heroic efforts be taken to save the life of a baby who may need continual medical care throughout its life? Should healthy people have operations to donate organs? When is an operation just too expensive to justify its use? The Park Ridge Center in Chicago is one place where doctors and theologians are coming together to find ways to resolve these questions. They also work to encourage treatment of the body, mind, and spirit as a whole.

◈◈◈◈◈

CHAPTER FOUR

BELIEF SYSTEMS AND HEALTH

Contributors:

Rachel Naomi Remen, M.D., is the Medical Director of the Commonweal Cancer Help Program in Bolinas, California.

Leonard Duhl, M.D., is a psychiatrist at the University of California in Berkeley and San Francisco. He has been involved for the past five years with the "Healthy Cities" project of the World Health Organization, and with Unicef on the Distressed Urban Child project.

Harriet Beinfield, L.Ac., an acupuncturist, Chinese herbalist, and the co-author of *Between Heaven and Earth,* studied Chinese medicine in England and China. She is a co-founder of the Chinese Medicine Works clinic in San Francisco.

Helene S. Smith, Ph.D., and **Andrew Weil, M.D.** (see bios on page 1)

◈ ◈ ◈

RACHEL NAOMI REMEN: The questions that interest me the most are not "Who has access to health care?" and "How do we achieve access for all people?" which seem to be the questions that are in most people's mind. As soon as those are resolved, the next question is the much more difficult one in some ways, which is: "Access to what? What is health care, and what is effective health care?" One of the interesting things that's happening, of course, is that we have in the last ten years reconceived what a health-care provider is. It used to be that if you had heart disease, the health-care provider was your cardiologist. Now, of course, you yourself, the individuals themselves, are seen as health-care providers.

I think that there is even yet a third step beyond either the expert, the medical expert as the health-care provider, or the individuals themselves, and that lies in recognition that healing is generally a work of relationship, that ordinary people heal one another, and that we are health-care providers for each other. People have been healing each other since the beginning, long before there were physicians, long before there were CAT scanners, long before there were MRIs, long before there were experts. Healing is part of our birthright as human beings, and as we come closer to our essential nature, we become aware that that nature can heal both ourselves and other people.

Of course, then, the job site, the school, the church, anyplace that people gather becomes a means of healing. If "it takes a whole village to raise a child," perhaps it may take a whole community to ensure the health of any of its members, and the American people themselves may be the great health providers of the future.

LEONARD DUHL: It's quite clear that as you get into the urban communities, you will find that they are made up of tremendously diverse populations, and these diverse populations, all of them, use various kinds of what we now would call alternative practices. So you'll find Chinese medicine, and you'll find *curanderos* [healers]. You'll find all these people. Most of the cities' health programs, at least the official ones, are run with a Western standard model. But the truth is that most populations use both kinds of models. So I think that it's really tremendously important that we begin to look more and more at these alternative models, see how well they work and how they don't work.

In some instances, we know that populations choose between traditional medical solutions and different kinds of care. They will choose, in the Chinese community—for certain chronic illnesses—to go for Chinese medicine, but for certain things that Western does very well, they'll go to Western physicians. We find even a new group of professionals who will help people go between these two worlds. We see them in the *curanderos,* and some in the Hispanic communities and the like. I'm very excited about what's happening now.

I have very strong feelings about the fact that people must participate in their own healing, whether it's on an individual level or a community level. You can't ask somebody just to "do to you" and expect things to happen. With a lot of Western medicine, the expectation is that I can passively sit back and let something be done to me so I'll be well. But more and more, we know that the mind, the attitude, the environment, and the context changes the internal human being and aids and assists in the process of healing or, in fact, hinders the process of healing. So I think the involvement is tremendously important. I do not think that you can blame a person for becoming ill, or blame a person for not getting well. But there has to be an active collaboration and partnership between the various people who are involved, including the patient.

MICHAEL TOMS: *The whole theory of disease in the Chinese system is different from the Western allopathic model. Could you tell us how it's different and why it's different?*

HARRIET BEINFIELD: The allopathic theory is based on Cartesian logic, which breaks the body into smaller and smaller constituent parts. Descartes thought that the universe could be conceived as a well-made clock, and that everything that was real could be seen, measured, touched. And, in fact, what was not seen needed to be separated from the material. So the mind became separated from the body, and disease became an entity that you could separate from the person who has it. Pathogens were isolated from the disease process as a whole. And symptoms could be viewed separately from the source of the ailment. So, in effect, doctors became mechanics who treated the body, which was viewed as a machine, and replaced and fixed broken body parts. So that came to be who doctors were.

In the Chinese view or cosmology, the body is seen as a little miniature universe, a microcosm of nature. And the metaphors are poetic, natural metaphors. So the body is an ecosystem, and the job of the doctor is like a gardener whose job is to cultivate the landscape, balancing the elements of heat and cold, wetness and dryness. And the function of the physician is very different. In fact, there's a legend that the Chinese physician was only compensated, was only paid to keep the body healthy, and if the body became sick, that showed an incompetence on the part of the physician. So, in Chinese medicine, the doctor is a gardener whose job is to cultivate the health of the organism and maintain the harmony and balance within the ecosystem.

So the languages are very different. Whereas Western medicine focuses on the problem, the pathogen, the tumor, in Chinese medicine the focus is on the person who has it, the host, and so the job of the physician is interpreted very differently.

MICHAEL: *It sounds like the Chinese system is more oriented to prevention than ours is. Is that true?*

HARRIET: It is, because it's possible to be treated, within the Chinese system, before you have any complaint.

And it's possible, by re-equilibrating and encouraging the self-regulatory part of the body, to avoid illness or to catch it in its earlier stages, before it becomes deeply entrenched and problematic.

MICHAEL: *And how about the healer—the doctor or the healer?*

LEONARD: As you may remember, the ancient healers and the shamans are complex people. They were people who were spiritual leaders; they were people who were community leaders. They were also actual doctors and healers of the body. Most of the things that I understand about it, about the way they worked, involved people in their own healing process. When somebody gave birth, you got the father to boil the water, you got the people in the community involved in the process. And so the healer, healer/shaman, even the modern doctor should be somebody who orchestrates those processes, and has to have a commitment to the participation, and has to get deeply involved with the patient. In fact, I'd even go further and say that in most instances where I'm most successful with patients, and I still see patients, I'm never sure whether I'm there just to heal the patient, or is something coming from the patient to heal me at the same time?

ANDREW WEIL: Helene has spoken of doctors and shamans and the need to turn out more shamans. Now we come back to that as a practical possibility—how do we do that more? The ideas of community referred to here, I think, are very important. There are more and more research studies that make it look as if a community connection often overrides obvious physical variables such as diet, exercise or lack of it, and smoking. A famous study was done in Pennsylvania, in a town and community where the older generation did not have very good health habits, but had a very low rate of cardiovascular disease. But the second generation that lived there had the same health habits, but had lost the extended family sense, so their rates of cardiovascular disease rose very quickly to equal those of other American communities. Those kinds of studies are very important. It's not just what vitamins you take and what foods you eat, but how connected you are to other people. Altruism often shows up as a constant theme in people who are healthy as well as successful.

HELENE: I'd like to return to science. I think there's a danger in all of this glorifying of alternatives. Although I respect them tremendously, there's a danger in having people use an herb or some other alternative the same way they would use an aspirin. We, first of all, need to question whether sometimes these herbs may not be effective as in Western medicine, and that there are two different issues. One is what the mind believes and how that impacts on wellness, and the other is a particular medicine that changes the physiology. I think many of these alternatives need to be studied from a scientific perspective as well.

ANDREW: I certainly agree with that, and I think the ideal treatment is one which intrinsically produces an effect in the direction that you want, as verified by experimental method, and is also presented to a patient in a way that maximally engages their belief system in the service of healings.

◈ ◈ ◈

SUMMARY

Our belief systems have a profound effect on our health. They determine how we take care of our health, when we seek medical treatment, and to whom we go for that treatment. If we believe that doctors know everything and a doctor tells us that further care is hopeless, we may give up and preclude any chance of cure or healing. On the other hand, people have had "miraculous" cures attributed to their beliefs that cure was possible through divine intervention, or through their own will to live. Researchers have noted that certain belief systems may make us more susceptible to diseases such as cancer. We inherit belief systems from our families and cultural backgrounds, altering them as we educate ourselves throughout our lives. People from the many different cultures that make up this country look for medical treatments that fit their belief systems. Today some medical practices are exploring ways to better fulfill these needs.

◈◈◈◈◈

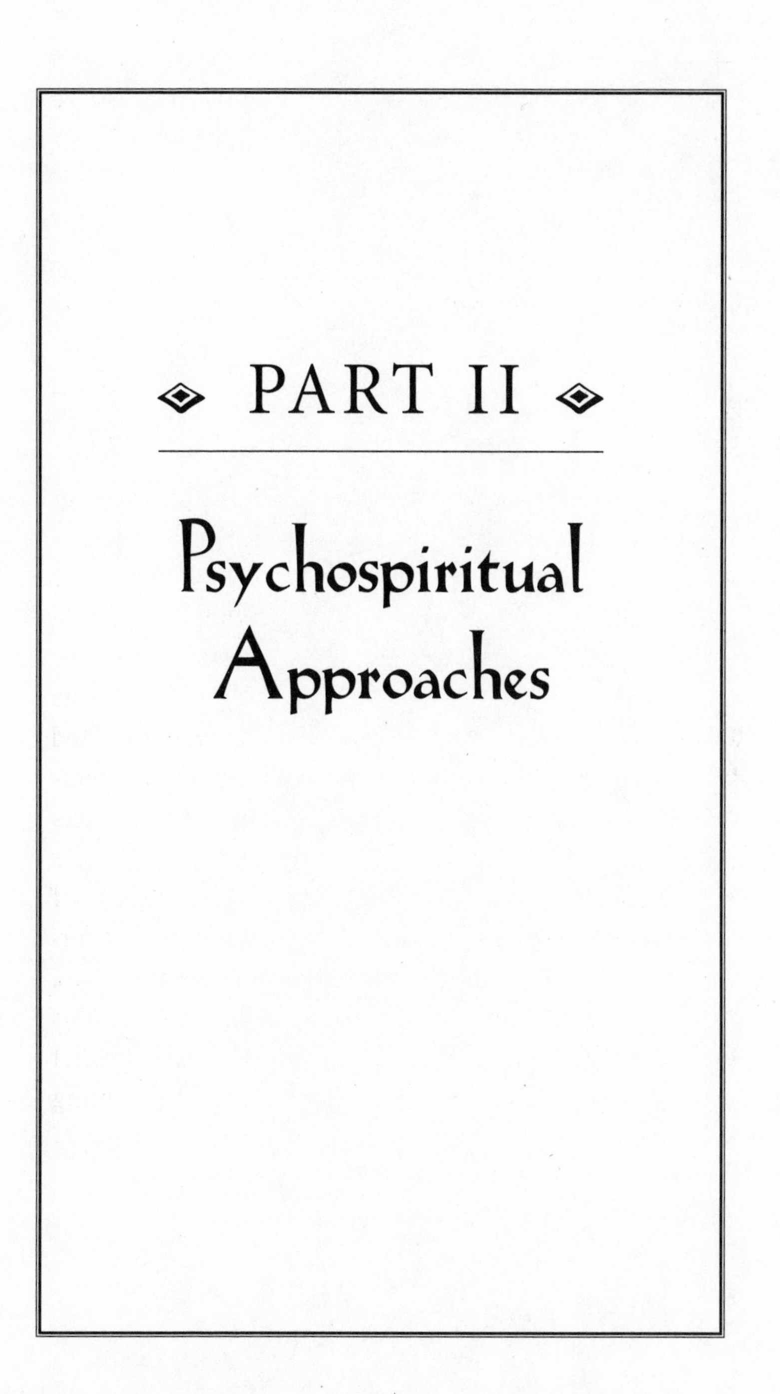

PART II

Psychospiritual Approaches

CHAPTER FIVE

Alternative Therapies for Heart Disease and Cancer

Contributors:

The late **Rev. Barbara St. Andrews** co-founded and served as Executive Director of Medicine and Philosophy for the California Pacific Medical Center. A priest with training in Comparative Spirituality and Healing, she did extensive pastoral work with AIDS and cancer patients. She is the author of the book, *Ripening in the Wilderness,* to be published posthumously (Barbara died in an auto accident in April 1994).

Michael Lerner, Ph.D., is the founder of the Commonweal Cancer Help Program in Bolinas, California, a series of week-long stress reduction, health education, and group support workshops for cancer patients and their families. He also works with adolescent offenders.

Marion Weber, M.A., of the Healing Arts Center, Stinson Beach, California, is a dancer, artist, and Art Director of the Commonweal Cancer Help Program.

James Duke, Ph.D., is an economic botanist for the U.S. Department of Agriculture and a highly regarded authority on botanical medicines. He has done field work in the Amazon basin and has produced 15 books on economic botany.

Rachel Naomi Remen, M.D. (see bio on page 33)
Andrew Weil, M.D. (see bio on page 1)

***MICHAEL TOMS:** Cardiovascular disease is the number-one killer in America today, followed by cancer, which claims one in five Americans each year. How do we deal with these two threats? More specifically, how do we live with them? There are a multitude of ways we've been conditioned to perceive heart disease and cancer. They parallel the high-tech ways medicine has developed to treat these illnesses. However, there are those who are expanding the territory and giving us new tools to address cancer and heart disease while enhancing the quality of life.*

So, heart disease and cancer, the two big killers in America today—where are we with these relatively new approaches?

ANDREW WEIL: First of all, I think we are seeing a lot of admission within the medical profession that prevention is key with these diseases, that treatments for these diseases, once they're established, are unsatisfactory and probably are going to remain so for a while. But in general, these are diseases of lifestyle; they're diseases that have environmental causes or are rooted in habits of eating, handling stress, exercising or not exercising, which can be corrected, and if people took corrective action early enough in life, we would have a much lower incidence of these diseases. So I think we're beginning to see some emphasis on real preventive education and incentives for people to improve lifestyle.

BARBARA ST. ANDREWS: I think these are also diseases that have psychological and spiritual components, and they relate to the meaning system of the individual and the family. So it's increasingly important to look at the whole person in order to have healing take place, not just curing in the strictly medical sense.

ANDREW: Certainly with heart disease, I think it's no accident that we refer to having "broken hearts" and heart pains in our hearts and heartthrobs to describe our state of emotional relation to other people. And I think the physical heart is very sensitive to those kinds of emotional considerations. That's an issue that has tended not to be looked at by medicine that simply focused on the physical body.

BARBARA: I've been reading the life story of Catherine of Aragon, Henry VIII's first wife. I read when they did the autopsy following her death, they found a large black mass surrounding her heart, which 19th-century physicians said was a melanotic sarcoma, but even in that day they had a sense of the connection between the mind and the spirit, because she had a life that was really a profound sense of grief. So the connection between the emotional state of the patient and the disease that manifests is very intimate.

ANDREW: You used the phrase "mind and the spirit," Barbara, and today I think it's very fashionable to talk about "mind/body medicine" and "mind/body connection," but often spirit is left out of that formula.

BARBARA: I think that's a very limited perspective, because if you look it up in the dictionary, *mind* and *spirit* come under *psyche,* which even has mythological implications, whereas the body itself—sarks, matter—is informed or illuminated by the spiritual and psychological components. They interact; they intersect.

ANDREW: In Buddhism, also, the term *mind,* which is used frequently, really includes what we in the West refer to as *heart.* It refers to all the emotional aspects of a human being, all the feelings, as well as simply intellectual functions and thought.

BARBARA: It comes back to the spiritual issue, because there are elements that can't be seen. You can see the heart, but you can't see the emotions, just as you can't witness love, and you can't hold it in your hand. One of the difficulties in contemporary medicine is that we've tended to value that which was more matter-oriented, and so we pay the surgeon more than the psychiatrist, and certainly more than the chaplain, which says something about the value system from which we operate.

ANDREW: My experience is that Western medicine has really greatly limited its effectiveness and understanding of disease processes by focusing only on the material aspects of human beings. If we think that all disease results from material causes, or that any change in the physical body has to have a material cause, that cuts us off from seeing a whole realm of causation where we could make positive changes to affect a person's life.

BARBARA: I think this is an historic controversy, because, from a theological point of view, a Buddhist would talk about "beginner's mind," and other world religions would have a perspective that encompasses a beginning with the idea. This is Platonic, as opposed to the Aristotelian idea that you either emphasize matter or you emphasize the idea. Coming from a theological perspective, just one instance can give one a perspective—one trip across the Red Sea, one individual coming back to life, whatever it is—can set a metaphor from which one can operate, whereas in medicine there's a tendency to go for the double-blind study or the replicable reality, so is it inductive or deductive predominantly in one's thinking?

MICHAEL TOMS: *[I think one of the places where some new approaches, particularly to the treatment of cancer, are being used is the Commonweal Cancer Help Program in Bolinas, California.]*

There's a lot of misinformation out there regarding alternative cancer therapies and their effectiveness. You've [Michael Lerner] done a lot of research in this area. Have you found any miraculous cancer cures in the whole complementary medicine area?

MICHAEL LERNER: I've looked at hundreds of complementary cancer therapies. My basic conclusions have stayed the same, which are, first, that there is no cure for any specific cancer among the alternative cancer therapies. And second, there's very little scientific evidence on which to evaluate the really interesting question, which is not whether there's a cure, but whether some people do well on these therapies. In the same way, many chemotherapies are not a cure, but extend life, for example, so that using the criterion of "cure" is not really a fair criterion, given how difficult it is to cure many cancers.

So the second point is that there is very little evidence from which to assess that for the complementary therapies, whether they help. The third point is that there is strong anecdotal evidence that some people *do* do well, apparently, on these therapies, but we don't have science to know whether that's within the normal range or not.

The fourth point is that while the war continues in the trenches between the true believers in unconventional therapies and the true believers that all unconventional therapies are quack treatments of no value, there is a growing middle ground of informed clinicians and researchers on both sides of these issues who are saying to each other, "Look, there's no point in fighting about this. There's plenty of room for improvement and genuine therapies for cancer patients on both sides. So let's talk together, and let's find a middle ground of dialogue in research." I'm frankly very uninterested in the sort of lobbing back and forth of grenades on these issues. I'm interested in that middle ground.

On that middle ground, for example, when I started this field, it was heresy to suggest that psychological interventions might extend life with cancer. Now there are two controlled studies indicating, with breast cancer and with malignant melanoma, that in fact it may have a very dramatic effect on life extension—not cure, but life extension—with metastatic cancers.

For how many cancers may this turn out to be true? We don't have the information. More than that, what happens if it's not just a psychological intervention? What happens if people improve their diets? What happens if they're using traditional Chinese medicine? What happens if they're going to a healer who's a reputable healer? Is there a cascade effect of all these things coming together that enhances resiliency forces and health-promotion forces within the person? And what are the outer limits? I don't think this is a cure. I think cancer is very difficult to cure once it's established, if it's a metastatic cancer. But I think that there's a very real possibility that when people look back 50 years ago from now, they will see our lack of attention to mental hygiene in cancer with the same horror that we look back on the lack of attention to physical hygiene of early surgeons who didn't wash their hands before surgery.

I'm just convinced that there are dimensions of this that are not fully explored scientifically yet, and if we approach it in a balanced way, we may learn some things that are genuinely helpful. There's no question that this includes quality of life in people with cancer. It's well demonstrated scientifically that psychological interventions, on a broad range of measures, improve quality of life. The question is, does it extend life? And I would suggest the evidence is increasing that, for some cancers at least, it *may* extend life as well.

BARBARA: I think he [Michael] raises an important issue about the quality of time one has versus the quantity. I can remember, as a young seminarian, standing in a darkened doorway of a chapel in a Washington hospital with a physician who had not told the patient that she had terminal cancer because he had ordered intensive chemotherapy. And I questioned that decision. He said, "If it were I in that circumstance, I'd rather be able to sit in a wheelchair in the window of the hospital than die." I said, "Perhaps this patient would rather go to Maui for a week and have some intensive time with her family. And is that not her decision?" So when we get into issues of extension of life, I'm sure we've been with people who have died under all kinds of circumstances, some pretty impossible. I think there's a great fear of extending life when it involves pain and suffering and misery. So these factors are extremely critical.

ANDREW: I also want to say, Michael, that while everyone surely is in favor of extending life with cancer, improving quality of life, using psychological interventions and other lifestyle adjustments if possible, we should not neglect the possibility that cures of cancer occasionally occur, even with metastatic cancer. I think it's very important to identify these cases and try to figure out what happened there. The Institute of Noetic Science Remissions Project identified thousands of reported cases of cancer cures in the medical literature. Science, medical science, has never looked in this direction. It's never looked at remission as a phenomenon. My feeling is that we're not going to find any neat correlation with any particular external treatment that was done. I think the significance of this is that it points to the fact that there is a healing potential within everyone that may operate very powerfully in some kinds of illnesses, and with other kinds of illnesses such as metastatic cancer, it may not operate very frequently. But when it does, it's very important to look at those individual cases, because I think that the more we focus on them, perhaps the more we can make that phenomenon happen.

BARBARA: The priest Andrew Greeley did a study that showed that people tend to tell other people what they believe the other people will believe. So the miraculous or the numinous, or the things that happen on a very high frequency level are often not reported or shared because there's a sense they wouldn't be believed.

ANDREW: What a physician believes and says to a patient has a major impact on the patient's belief system. It's very important to try to chip away at this pessimism among medical doctors about many forms of chronic illness, especially metastatic cancer. One way to do that is by encouraging the attention on cases of remission when they occur.

BARBARA: And much of this has a legal impetus, because if the physician's protecting himself or herself from possible liability by giving every potential side effect, what that is also doing is setting up in the patient both the fear that could happen and the increased probability. So it's toxic waste.

MARION WEBER: I always feel that we are rushed in our healing. Healing is not a rushed affair. It is something that needs to breathe and expand, and that's one thing I've learned in the work that I do. Therefore, our healing places are very uncomfortable for so many of us because they are not expansive places. What we try to create at Commonweal is really just a space in which healing can breathe, in which the healing juices can stir. So many of the people that come to us have been too rushed. I mean, that is really the big word I like to pull out there—too *rushed.* Let's just stop for a moment and listen, and begin the healing process.

RACHEL NAOMI REMEN: Technology is not a tool of healing; it's a tool of curing. Healing comes out of very simple human relationships, knowing your life matters to another person, connecting together to something larger and unseen. We heal each other all the time, we people, and we don't even value it. We don't even realize that we're doing it.

Our whole culture is oriented towards the doing, the acting, and not toward what might be considered the more feminine part of every human being—the receiving and the nurturing, the listening and the acknowledging of the uniqueness of each other. Yet being received as we are is what allows us to expand into who we are. It lifts off the social pressures, the self-expectations, the expectations of others, and says to them, without any words, "Be. Be here. Be alive. You are of value."

ANDREW: One comment I have, and I'm interested in Barbara's response to this—Rachel Naomi Remen mentioned feminine consciousness and its importance in healing. When I was a student at Harvard Medical School in the late 1960s, there were 12 women in my class, in a class of about 160. That has changed dramatically since then. The classes I teach at the University of Arizona now often have 51 percent women. But so far I haven't seen that make any difference in medicine. I think the problem is that for women to succeed in that system, they have to think like men, they have to disown their feminine consciousness. I wonder if the sheer presence of all those women in the profession will eventually produce a shift in the direction that we'd like to see.

BARBARA: I think that many of those women you're describing often have a psychic split. When they're in the hospital situation and they know what it takes to get ahead, they behave in the masculine way. But I find that more female physicians than male physicians have often sought my support or counsel, and there have been several who have asked me to pray with them before they've had their own babies, or they have had to make medical decisions. So I see often in these women, if they're affirmed, a capacity just to suspend into the *mysterium tremendum*—and to trust the nonquantifiable.

ANDREW: In many ways, I find nurses to be much more open to and in touch with the subject matter that we've been talking about in these programs, and yet nurses as professionals are so disempowered that they're not able to make much of a difference. I also find, in my own practice, that I have about 70 percent women, 30 percent men. I think this is the same figure that's reported by publishers of medical self-help books, that women are the greater buyers of those books.

BARBARA: I think it may even transcend gender, however, and be somewhat personality-based. I think people who are sensate thinkers tend to go into medicine more, whereas more of the intuitive feelers who are more emotional in nature tend to go into nursing. That's the one component of personality theory that does break out male-female, generally, but not always. I think what's happening, however, is that the more intuitive, feeling nurses, many of them, are leaving the medical institution for the same reason and going into massage therapy and other related complementary therapies, because they can't exist in the bureaucratic methodology.

MICHAEL LERNER: There is nothing specific to cancer in what we do. We just chose to do it with cancer, and then we developed the specific things that you need to know about doing it with cancer. But generically, this is a healing program, and generically, in fact, you don't have to be sick to in any way benefit from this kind of work. This is a work of self-exploration for anybody who has begun to contemplate the fact that they may die someday and that they may go through some pain and suffering on the way, and have they developed a map of the five areas?

First, are the choices you make in healing; second, are the choices you'd make in mainstream medicine; third, are the choices you'd make in complementary approaches; fourth, are the choices you'd make in pain control; and fifth, are the choices you'd make in dying. The way I say it to people, those five areas of healing, mainstream, complementary, pain control, and dying are the five areas that anybody in the second half of life should begin to open up and explore, and just knowing that there is skill, knowledge, choice, and control in each of those areas—whether you can change the direction of your disease or not—you can transform it, and there are things to know in each of those areas that can be profoundly useful to somebody going through that specific crisis.

I'm not a person who romanticizes the experience of cancer. It's not okay with me that people whom I care about get cancer. It's not okay with me that they die. The sadness, and I would even use the word *horror,* that people face when they have life-threatening illnesses and it's not the right time in their life to go, and they have small children and they have husbands or wives that they care about—we're talking about terrible stuff, you know, terrible stuff. And the pain of that terrible stuff is very real. I can't escape from that suffering.

At the same time, there is a very old spiritual truth that pain can bring light. There is no question that in the Cancer Help Program, when people explore their pain together, and it's true pain, there is also light that emerges. But it doesn't erase the pain, so they are left holding, in their lives, both the pain and the light. I feel that it does them a disservice if we talk about all the beauty of the light without also talking about the pain.

ANDREW: In some ways, I think, cancer is the hardest disease to tackle, because the natural rate of remission is so low once it's established in the body. I meet many practitioners of therapies like visualization therapy, hypnotherapy, other kinds of mind/body interventions, who jump right into cancer. I usually tell them, "Why don't you wait? Why don't you first practice on allergy, autoimmunity conditions where remission is the rule rather than the exception? Or skin disorders, digestive disorders, where you can do a tremendous amount of good, especially since the conventional therapies in these areas are suppressive and toxic? And then, once you sharpen your teeth on those conditions, you know, then you can try cancer."

BARBARA: That makes me think of Agnes Sanford, who was a famous healer. She said, "There are two solutions for any known problem, and one is discernible by science, and one is discernible by faith." In circumstances of extreme nature, and listening to you and to Michael, it reminded me of one such situation. To bring hope, to bring any sign of light into a situation of darkness is transformative, and to me that's the critical thing, not that any of us has the cure, the answer for anyone else, but just to be open. The one patient who came to mind, I went down to Stanford Hospital on a rainy night, and she was drinking organic apple juice, which I thought was ironic given that she had a very serious liver cancer, and the physicians had told her if she stopped the chemotherapy cocktail she would die within about four days. She said to me as I left that night, "There's something I need to say to you, and I don't know what it is." As I turned around she said, "I need to say, 'I love you.'"

She called me a few days later. She'd checked herself out of the hospital and gone home. She asked me if I would come with any other people who had a spiritual belief and work with her. We used Lawrence LeShan's methods of visualization whereby you see the merging of yourself with the individual, like two birds in the sky, two trees on the horizon. When I got up from kneeling beside her with my hand on her solar plexus, I had a visualization of green, which to me was a sign of healing. To make a long story short, she lived for four months. She wrote a letter to everyone she loved. She had marvelous interactions with her children. One day when I was there praying with her, she asked me to pray that she would have the strength to sit up, and afterwards I brought her a cup of tea. And it wasn't until I was driving down the driveway from her home that I said to myself, "My God, she was sitting up when I left." She died a week after Easter, but on Easter she went to the Fairmont Hotel in a new dress she'd bought and had Easter dinner with her family. When she finally died, on the day I buried her, the text of the day was, "Father, into thy hands I place my spirit." Her life wasn't taken from her by either the medical system or the terminus of her disease. I think she transcended it, so the meaning of the whole thing was very hopeful even though the outcome was very tragic. And this happens every day. It's participating in it with some vision.

MICHAEL TOMS: *Jim, you did an interview with* East-West *magazine—I think it's now called* Natural Health. *And I quote you, if I'm right: "Vegetable soup offers more promise in reducing mortality from cancer than do present medicines, synthetic or natural." Can you expand on that?*

JAMES DUKE: My point there was that prevention was much better than cures...I have reason to suspect that the body can reach into a soup or an herb tea and pull out compounds that it needs, and exclude compounds that it doesn't need. Now, this is going a long way from what's been shown for selenium. But when the body needs selenium, it really can grab it out of an herb tea. When the body is getting too much selenium, that is to say, you've eaten 50 Brazil nuts and your hair starts falling out, the body homeostatically develops mechanisms to exclude this selenium. So, by this process of homeostasis, the human body, which has evolved with these soups and teas and not with these silver bullets, has mechanisms in many cases for grabbing what it wants and for excluding what it doesn't want. I think the body's smarter than the physicians give it credit for being.

MICHAEL TOMS: *What does this philosophy and approach, and your incredible knowledge about plant medicines, have to do with the major diseases that we've been discussing—heart disease, cancer, and even AIDS?*

JIM: I think anytime you can replace meat with beans, you'll lessen your chances of cancer and heart disease, especially if your beans are well spiced with onions and garlic and carrots...For AIDS, I'm encouraged to think that there are at least three anti-retroviral compounds. An herb that I know is St. John's Wort, or some people call it St. Peter's Wort, and that lies behind my quacky, flaky old All-Saint's Tea, in which I mix up several species of hypericum, each of which contain at least two anti-retroviral compounds, and one of which contains a monoamine oxidase inhibitor. And these, I think, can help with depression, so there's a double whammy against the AIDS virus there.

On the diabetic front, I think diet can help a whole lot in stage two, or late-onset diabetes, especially, again, the beans in the diet. And there are lots of spices and herbs that can treble the efficiency of insulin.

I've seen a lot of good evidence that flax can help in the prevention of cancer, the lignans [sic] that are therein.

And I certainly would not discourage it. There are other equally good sources of alpha-linoleic acid. But I think I don't want to get anybody eating all beans or all flax or all cabbage or all garlic. I want them to eat a variety of beans, a variety of garlic varieties, a variety of onion varieties. Variety is the spice of life and may be the salvation of life.

BARBARA: I love the spirit of Jim Duke. He's a colorful anomaly in institutional bureaucracy, which we need more of, and he's also making efforts to train physicians in the natural sources of drugs as opposed to the synthetic, as you're doing, Andrew.

ANDREW: I'm a big fan of botanical medicine and nutritional medicine. Taxol, from the Pacific yew, is the same old thing. It's just another variation on a cell poison and it, along with all other varieties of chemotherapies, I predict, will be obsolete within 20 to 30 years. I think a lot of new holistic methods of treating cancer will emerge, rather than our current methodologies of trying to poison cancer cells.

Like Jim, I'm also very excited about genistein from soy. There is reason to think that soy and a number of other plants, carrots among them, have substances called phytoestrogens. These are estrogen-like compounds that may interact with the estrogen receptors in cells, but they might only weakly activate those receptors, and thus prevent them from being occupied by the body's natural estrogen or, more importantly, perhaps, by a number of external substances artificially produced, like DDT and other pollutants. We're beginning to think that external substances artificially produced might strongly act with the estrogen receptor and might be the reason for the worldwide increase in breast cancer.

I found out recently that Japanese women have very low rates of breast cancer, and Japanese men have low rates of prostate cancer. These low rates of these types of cancers might be due to the high Japanese consumption of soy products, rather than to a low-fat diet, which was thought previously. I also found that the Japanese women don't tend to get hot flashes in menopause.

ANDREW: I'd like to conclude by saying that I'm a big fan of the health-care crisis. It's really the only thing which is producing open-mindedness in medicine today. If medicine were not in the kind of economic trouble it is right now, it would be business as usual. All these alternative approaches we've been talking about would continue to be denigrated as nonsense and unscientific. But the ship is really sinking, hospitals are on the verge of bankruptcy, the insurance system is breaking down, and given that situation, there is real desperation in medicine. In their desperation, doctors, for the first time in a century, are being willing to consider other ways of doing things. I think there is a real chance right now to create new kinds of institutions, to take care of sick people. There's a real chance to make reforms of medical education that are more than just shuffling medical training courses around. There's a real chance to begin creating new kinds of health professionals and eventually to change the model and paradigm that's in place at the moment in Western science and medicine.

◈ ◈ ◈

SUMMARY

For much of the 20th century, modern medicine has focused on the scientific approach to curing diseases. Patients' psychological and spiritual states were seen as irrelevant to their bodies' condition. More recently, we have begun to realize that body, mind, and spirit are an interrelated parts of the whole, and that treatments need to take each of these aspects into account. A study recently published on patients with Lou Gehrig's Disease showed that those with psychological well-being were almost seven times as likely to survive during the three-year study period as those in a state of psychological distress. Studies by other doctors have shown that support-group work can extend the length of life while enhancing the quality of life for people with breast cancer and melanoma, and that comprehensive lifestyle changes including diet and stress reduction can reverse blockages in arteries. There is increasing evidence that multidimensional treatments that include body, mind, and spirit will prove the most effective treatment for many different diseases.

While researchers constantly seek cures for cancer and heart disease, they are also looking for ways to prevent these diseases. James Duke, one of the foremost authorities in the U.S. on the medicinal uses of plants, says that the genistein found in soybeans, red clover, and several other legumes has been shown to prevent the formation of new blood vessels to newly developing cancerous tumors, and also shows anti-hypertensive activity. He says that replacing meat with beans lessens your chances of cancer and heart disease, especially if the beans are well spiced with onions, garlic, and carrots, each of which has medicinally useful components. Low rates of breast and prostate cancer in Japanese people are thought to be attributable to their diet. Japanese women also tend not to get hot flashes during menopause. Anti-retroviral compounds in St. John's Wort and other hypericums may be helpful to people with AIDS. Many other medicinal uses are being found for common plants, but drug companies have no incentive to spend the approximately $357,000 required to prove a new drug effective unless they are able to secure a proprietary interest. This may tend to minimize research on plant-derived medicines.

◈◈◈◈◈

CHAPTER SIX

The Relationship Between Attitude, Spirituality, and Homeopathy

Contributors:

Andrew Weil, M.D. (see bio on page 1)
Rev. Barbara St. Andrews (see bio on page 43)
Daniel Goleman, Ph.D. (see bio on page 2)

ANDREW WEIL: Barbara, you've worked in a major medical center in the San Francisco area, and I wonder what that experience was like. I occasionally give lectures to the pastoral care staff at the University of Arizona hospital, and in general I find them to be a dispirited group.

I think it must be very difficult to be in a small minority of people who hold a different paradigm, working in a temple of scientific materialism.

BARBARA ST. ANDREWS: Absolutely true. If you're female in that context, it's even more interesting. I think what's happening in medical centers which is hopeful, however, is that the more the respect grows between the physician and the spiritual healer, the shaman is re-created. When I first went to that medical center, if I arrived at the doorway of a patient's room at the same time as the physician, there was no question who would go in first. By the time I left, there would be a very short pause, and the patient would decide. I think that's what makes the difference—where in the meaning system, and how do we complement one another to get to whatever the objective is? When I was a really green priest—I've been in the ministry 14 years now, but back in the beginning—I remember saying to a nurse, "When a patient dies, is the body heavier or lighter?" I had no idea. And she said, "Well, you know that expression, 'dead weight'? The body's lighter when it's alive." I thought, it's the spirit that enlivens and enlightens.

That same spirit is in the healers of all different stripes, whatever we are. One of the things in scripture that Jesus asked Peter was, "Do you love me?" I think that's the underlying question in life, in every encounter, and it's the same question between the priest and the doctor. From my point of view, the best way to change things is to do it at the level of medical education. If that respect could be engendered while we're in training, I think the system could really change.

ANDREW: I agree, and I have a strong commitment to try to do that. But I also recognize the inertia and weight of the current model. Scientific materialism denies the reality or importance of nonphysical factors. That's why homeopathy is so incomprehensible to standard medicine. You know, homeopathic medicine really is a kind of spiritual medicine; instead of using the material aspect of a drug, you're using the spiritual essence of a drug to affect the vibrational state of the body. That makes no sense to a chemist or somebody trained in chemistry and physics.

ANDREW: What do we do about this? I mean, acupuncture has been tremendously accepted in this culture because it involves sticking needles into people, which is physical, even though it comes from a system that's very different in its philosophy. But homeopathy is still very much on the outs.

BARBARA: And yet during the cholera epidemic, the homeopathists had much better results than the allopathic physicians.

ANDREW: I think we're going to see, in the next century, the evolution of a new field of energy medicine, which will develop new scientific models that might be able to explain homeopathy. But that will really be the paradigm shift, when that happens.

BARBARA: Well, even beyond homeopathy, imagine if your tool is prayer, if that's what you're carrying into the room. If we look for a validation from external sources, it would be discouraging.

ANDREW: Yes. This is a system of alternative medicine that dates back to the late 1700s, invented by a very spiritual German physician named Samuel Hahnemann, that's based on giving very, very tiny doses of highly diluted natural substances which, if given to normal people, reproduce the symptoms of illness. It's a system that is practiced by many people of very different kinds of training. There are some M.D.'s who do it today, there are naturopaths who do it, chiropractors; you can buy homeopathic remedies in health food stores. It's a system that is very prominent in England and countries of Europe and India, and is increasing in popularity again in this country.

BARBARA: If you can accept the premise that energy exchanges, and the further premise that love is a healing ingredient, you can see that same phenomenon in other, subtle ways. I can remember taking a 10-year-old boy who had leukemia to see a 50-year-old man with leukemia, and then I stood in the door. I heard the child say to the man, "Look, George, I went through this, It's hell. If I can do it, you can do it." Afterwards, the 50-year-old man said to me, "That's the most valuable healing I received in this medical center." It's an exchange of an intangible.

ANDREW: I see so many patients who are victims of this kind of thing, who are told in one way or another that they're not going to get better, that they're going to die. Some of these stories are just horrific. I had a woman in her mid-50s who had metastatic ovarian cancer, was in a very bad relationship with her oncologist, and kept telling the oncologist she was going to beat the odds on this thing. He said no, she wasn't. One day she insisted she was going to survive, and he said, "Look, the only way you're not going to die of your cancer is if you get hit by a truck." That finally motivated her to get another oncologist.

This happens so often. I wonder where it comes from. Why are doctors so pessimistic about healing? That seems very strange, you know? If you're going to go into the healing arts, you ought to believe that healing is possible. I wonder about this. Some of it is that they're not taught it, that we don't study remission and so forth, but I think there may be a very deep psychological motivation for this. When you think about why people go into medicine, often we hear that people go into it for money or for prestige. I think there's a very deep psychological motivation that draws many people into medicine, and that is that it provides an illusion of control over life and death. Deep down, physicians know that they don't have control over life and death. Every time a patient fails to get better, or dies, it's a very stark reminder of the fact that you don't have control over life and death. As a way of protecting themselves psychologically and making it more comfortable for themselves, it may be easier for doctors to make these negative predictions—because then, if the patient does get better, what a nice surprise, and it reinforces the illusion, but if the patient dies, you haven't lost anything.

BARBARA: The health of the physician is tied in here, too. I mean the psychic and spiritual health. I remember a study by the Robert Wood Johnson Foundation that showed that people who go into medicine tend to be among the healthier people as they go in: they don't smoke, and they don't stay up a lot at night, and that sort of thing. They're physically fit. By the time they come out of medical school, they're not in such great shape. So it's hard to teach someone else what you haven't learned yourself. The saying "Physician, heal thyself" comes from a very logical place.

ANDREW: So here again, the need is to really change the way we produce doctors.

BARBARA: But in terms of cancer and heart disease, which we've been discussing, I think this assertiveness may be the learning curve for cancer patients, who often tend to be tremendously nice people who have difficulty expressing either aggression or anger, and the learning curve for heart-care practitioners, where often the aggressiveness comes more easily than the gentleness. They're both imploding as opposed to exploding diseases.

DANIEL GOLEMAN: It's very interesting, the medical implications of pessimism. They're terrible. There's some very inspiring research that shows that people who are optimistic, who are hopeful, do better medically compared to people who are pessimistic, rather dramatically. I remember a study of people going for some really very severe surgery that involved taking out the marrow and replacing the marrow in the bones. It's a last-ditch kind of surgical procedure. The people who were optimistic going into that had something like three times the survival rate of the people who were pessimistic. They're finding that, across the span of disease, that there's something about the biology of hope that is beneficial. So you could say that the skepticism and pessimism that reigns is toxic thinking.

◈ ◈ ◈

SUMMARY

Some doctors and hospitals have patient-centered care in which you are encouraged to actively participate in your own care. Some, however, still use the model that the doctors and staff know what is needed and that the patient's job is just to accept what is being done to and for them. In any health-care setting, there are ways for individuals to become more involved in their own care. Some health-care professionals recommend that people be assertive in asking questions about their care, particularly if something appears to be wrong with their treatment or medication. Usually this can be done with humor, or simply with sincerity. It has also been suggested that expressing anger appropriately in defense of yourself, if necessary, can be very helpful.

Your attitudes also affect your health. Some studies have shown that truly optimistic people heal better than those who are pessimistic, perhaps because the optimistic person will take concrete steps to build health, while a pessimistic person may feel that there's no use to even try. Care needs to be taken, however, that one doesn't get fixated on any one emotion, or try to create false optimism. Anger can also be healing.

PART III

Changing Perceptions of Complementary Therapy

CHAPTER SEVEN

Complementary Medicine: Today and Tomorrow

Contributors:

Joe Jacobs, M.D., M.B.A., is the Director of the Office of Alternative Medicine at the National Institute of Health, recently approved by Congress to evaluate the effectiveness of alternative medical treatments.

Barbara Bernie, C.A., is the founder of the American Foundation of Traditional Chinese Medicine. She studied acupuncture in London and was instrumental in securing its legalization in California. She was diagnosed with ovarian cancer and opted to travel to China for a combination of Eastern and Western treatments, resulting in total remission.

Andrew Weil, M.D. (see bio on page 1)

◈ ◈ ◈

MICHAEL TOMS: *A third of all Americans seek relief from aches and pains outside mainstream medicine, spending $14 billion a year on such therapies as massage, biofeedback, and herbal medicine, suggests a survey conducted by Dr. David Eisenberg of Boston's Beth Israel Hospital and published in the* New England Journal of Medicine. *In all, Americans made 425 million visits to such providers in 1990, more than the 388 million visits to all family doctors, internists, and other primary health-care physicians combined. Clearly, Americans are seeking alternatives in greater and greater numbers. There is a hunger for more personal treatment, and a need for greater sensitivity in the healing process. Complementary medicine is upon us like a wave. Lest we be engulfed by the great variety of available alternatives, it is important to separate the wheat from the chaff, to focus on what's useful and what's not.*

So, let me ask you, Andrew and Barbara: Where do you think complementary medicine is today, and where is it going?

ANDREW WEIL: More and more Americans are turning to these alternative therapies in place of, or in combination with, regular medicine. This is a cycle that began, I think, at the end of the 1960s, and I think we're nowhere near the crest of this wave. If you look historically, interest in these alternatives has waxed and waned over long cycles depending on how well the public perceives standard medicine as doing its job. In the early part of this century, from 1900 to 1960, most people were captivated by scientific, technological medicine, and there was a real belief in this culture that science and technology were going to solve all of our problems, eventually doing away with disease and maybe death itself.

Somewhere around 1960, the technological dream began to fade, and as we began to see that science and technology created as many problems as they solved, this was when this present cycle began, of interest in alternatives. We're really well under way in that at the moment.

BARBARA BERNIE: Yes, and we have found tremendous interest over the last 22 years. Twenty-two years ago, when I became interested in it, seeking a method of treatment other than Western medicine—which was unable to take care of my problem—I had no place to go because it was against the law at that time to practice traditional Chinese medicine anywhere in the United States. So I had to go to Canada. At that time, traditional Chinese medicine was considered voodoo medicine and had great skeptics as to the interest in it and also the practice of it. Now we see a tremendous surge of interest and, of course, now we do have laws that allow for it as well.

ANDREW: I think the story of what's happened with traditional Chinese medicine in this country is astonishing. As Barbara said, not that long ago this was considered black magic. When I was a student at Harvard Medical School in the late sixties, acupuncture was put in the same category as sticking pins into voodoo dolls. That changed almost instantly when James Reston, the *New York Times* correspondent, had his appendix out on the front page of the *Times* while accompanying Nixon to China, and reported that acupuncture relieved his post-operative pain. Suddenly, as American doctors saw that American patients were willing to pay actual dollars for acupuncture, they suddenly took an interest in it. Now this has gone so far that in almost every town of any size in America, you can find someone practicing acupuncture in some form, or some form of Chinese medicine. This has really permeated our culture.

BARBARA: Our understanding of this whole medicine has expanded. It's not only acupuncture—it's herbs, it's diet, nutrition, it's special exercises, breathing exercises—it is also special types of massage that are therapeutic. So it's an expanded understanding of traditional Chinese medicine. Now, along with that, of course, we are learning about other types of healing that are complementary to Western medicine, such as homeopathy, Ayurvedic medicine, Tibetan medicine—and all of these have something to offer what we already have.

ANDREW: Of the various complementary therapies that you've mentioned, it's acupuncture that's had far greater acceptance in America. There are many M.D.'s who practice it; there are training programs for M.D.'s. It has become very accepted in standard hospitals as a treatment for pain. Yet, if you accept acupuncture, what you are accepting as a whole is a paradigm of medicine that's completely different from the Western paradigm that's based on ideas of energy circulation around the body.

Regarding imbalances of energy as causes of sickness, these ideas are very foreign to Western medicine. It's interesting that Western doctors are able to pick up that one piece of it and often not follow through with the implications, and yet you know they're very unwilling to deal with many of these other complementary therapies.

BARBARA: It's so interesting that you bring this up. Actually, the diagnosis of traditional Chinese medicine is very different from Western medicine, even though it is being used to a greater extent by physicians in some hospitals. Still, the diagnostic process needs to be understood if you really want to understand what is happening to the energy system of the person, because, in Chinese medicine, that's what we deal with. We say if the energy system is blocked or if it's out of balance, that's when the body breaks down and has disease. How do we find out about this energy system? We take pulses. There are 6 pulses on each wrist, and each pulse refers to a different organ in the body, and each pulse has 27 different qualities or characteristics. This is one of the ways that we can determine what is happening to the energy system, but it isn't the only way. We look at the tongue; the tip of the tongue tells us about the heart, the sides about the gall bladder/liver, the surface about the stomach/spleen, and so on and so forth. So we look at the skin, the eyes, the nails, the hair, and all of this, along with finding out about what the person is going through emotionally and also mentally and spiritually, in order to determine what the cause of the problem is. So even though a physician trained in Western medicine may be using it, if they haven't been trained in the total medicine, it's being used superficially.

MICHAEL: *So what we're talking about is that in many instances, acupuncture is being used with a Western diagnosis, and just the needles are being used to try and alleviate pain, but there isn't a total understanding of the system behind the use of the needles.*

ANDREW: Nonetheless, it's a foot in the door. What's attached to that foot is something very large, and that does not mesh with Western conceptions of reality. Even trying to talk about the energy system of the body with many Western doctors—it's very difficult to get that concept across. Now, they think you're talking mystical nonsense when you use words like *energy*.

JOE JACOBS: The purpose of the Office of Alternative Medicine is for the National Institute of Health [NIH] to fulfill a Congressional mandate to evaluate the clinical benefits that may be derived from various alternative medical treatments. Pure and simple.

There are several ways of doing it, one of which is to put out a solicitation for inviting people to apply for grant funds. We put out a solicitation, and we received over 800 letters of intent of people to apply, and finally got something like 460 grant applications, and eventually have selected 30 proposals for award.

MICHAEL: *Why do you see alternative medicine being important?*

JOE: In Dr. David Eisenberg's article that appeared in the *New England Journal of Medicine,* his survey showed that approximately 34 percent of the American public was using some form of alternative healing. He translated that into a national expenditure of about $13.5 billion. Irrespective of what methodological flaws might have existed in Dr. Eisenberg's study, it's still a lot of people, and a lot of money that's being expended on alternative healing practices.

I think what is very imperative for not only the NIH, but the entire medical community, is to engage the alternative practice of medicine not in a hostile manner, but in a collegial manner, to see what benefits can be derived out of these various alternative healing practices.

MICHAEL: *I notice that there are a number of persons you are working with in the office, one of whom is responsible for religion and spiritual issues having to do with healing.*

JOE: Right. I think this area is extremely important. The roots of it are clearly looking at the belief systems of patients. I think for far too long the conventional medicine has taken a very secular approach, for whatever reason, and either we don't understand religion and belief systems, or we don't want to understand religion and belief systems. I think the discipline of evaluation of alternative medicine mandates that we begin to look at the spirit and the role of spirituality in healing. Also, the role of that patient's belief systems, even if they translate into the placebo effect, needs to be explored.

MICHAEL: *What's implicit in all of this, it seems to me, is the aspect of rather than just depending on one form, we may be depending on multiple forms in the future. So we have the healer, the physician, and the therapist, all three, who are part of a health plan. What do you see?*

JOE: I can't say how that might translate into reimbursement, but I think from a conceptual point of view, as a clinician, as a person who works in primary care as opposed to medical research, I think I have a different view of how the health-care system deals with patients. It's multidimensional, yes, you're absolutely correct; you have to look at the various types of healing approaches. I think many of the concepts that we've learned in medical school are really not so much different from the quote, "Holistic approach to healing."

MICHAEL: *Do you see that a benefits package in the future could possibly include many alternative forms, provided they were scientifically validated?*

JOE: It depends upon the level of our knowledge of the clinical benefits that may be derived. I think we're already beginning to see movement in this area. If you look at Mutual of Omaha's recognition of Dr. Dean Ornish's treatment, the cardiac rehabilitation program, you're beginning to see people, at least organizations' payers, looking at the possible ways of being creative, of being able to incorporate these types of unconventional modalities as part of a benefits package. Clearly, if the data does show that, and experience bears it out, then Dean Ornish's program is a viable alternative to surgery or coronary angioplasty, or really a strong adjunct to medications for people with severe cardiovascular disease. I think you'll see a lot of activity toward incorporating that as part of a benefits package to the general public under health reform, after you've documented the clinical benefit.

But the imperative is, though, to provide good clinical data before you make that leap.

ANDREW: I have some comments on that. First of all, it seems to me that there's a much more important reason for looking at these therapies than simply that a lot of people are using them and spending a lot of money on them. I think a major reason why we should be looking in this direction is that conventional medicine is going down the tubes. It has become economically unworkable, and that's because of its reliance on high-technology solutions and external interventions to problems. The reason we should be looking in this direction is that there's a good chance that out there, in this world of complementary therapies, there are safer, more cost-effective methods of stimulating healing. While it's nice to say that what we might find in the holistic approach to healing is not all that different from what we've learned in medical school, I don't think that's the case. You know, in medical school I learned nothing about the natural healing power. You know, at the University of Arizona, where I teach, there's a big statue of Hippocrates right in the central courtyard of this vast complex. The two ideas of Hippocrates that are most remembered and most influential were first the statement that you should "First, do no harm" as a physician, and second that you should "Respect the healing power of nature." Both of those principles are consistently violated by conventional medicine today, and often are much more honored in some of these complementary therapies.

SUMMARY

Twenty years ago, practicing acupuncture in the United States was illegal. Now it is widely used here by both Western doctors and practitioners trained in other Chinese healing arts. These and other complementary therapies are gradually winning acceptance as both empirical and scientific evidence has grown about their effectiveness. The term *complementary* refers to the use of these therapies in conjunction with Western medical practices rather than being seen strictly as alternatives. As Dr. Daniel Goleman, editor of *Mind/Body Medicine*, said in a

New Dimensions interview, "Each of the methods of so-called 'alternative medicine' is only alternative until it's been tested and assessed as to whether it has a medical effect or it doesn't. And if it does, all of a sudden it's new medicine." The challenge has been to find funding and researchers willing to make these tests possible. We have much to learn from the methods and pharmacopoeia of traditional medicines such as Ayurveda, homeopathy, and acupuncture.

◈◈◈◈◈

CHAPTER EIGHT

New Approaches to Health Care: A Discussion

Contributors:

Sandra McLanahan, M.D., is an authority on preventive medicine, nutrition, and stress reduction. She is also an attending physician at the Richmond Center for Health and Wellness in Richmond, Virginia.

Robert Duggan, M.A., M.Ac., is a former Catholic priest and the President and Director of the Acupuncture Institute in Columbia, Maryland.

Vasant Lad, M.A. Sc., is a well-respected teacher and practitioner of Ayurvedic medicine and the author of several books on the subject of Ayurvedic philosophy and practice.

Andrew Weil, M.D. (see bio on page 1)
Barbara Bernie, C.A. (see bio on page 75)

MICHAEL TOMS: *I don't know if this story is apocryphal or if it's a myth or a mythic tale or what, but the story is that in ancient China, the doctors would only get paid if the patients were well. They only got supported if nobody got sick. It really is a different orientation, because in many respects, doctors are trained now that death is the enemy, and if you lose your patient to death, you've failed. We're really talking about having to get into the core and transform the basis of how doctors are trained, right?*

ANDREW WEIL: Absolutely. At the moment, the medical curriculum is entirely about disease. There's almost nothing in it about health and its maintenance, or real prevention. If you look at prevention, this takes you into major areas of social and political concern. For example, if it is true that the worldwide epidemic of breast cancer that we're seeing has a lot to do with pollutants in the environment, with chemicals like DDT and products of plastics manufacture, this raises enormous questions, such as, how do we change the society so we are not promoting disease?

BARBARA BERNIE: Yes, and what we are needing is a totally new approach to health care—to looking at it differently, to offering many more options of health care, and to informed consumers, who are understanding not only the different medicines that are out there, but how they affect them personally in their own health. Then patients can participate in their own health-care system and discuss these alternatives with the practitioner who is taking care of them. We hope to do this, in establishing an international health center in the San Francisco Bay Area.

MICHAEL: *Can you tell us a little more about the International Health Center?*

BARBARA: Actually, it was conceived 12 years ago, when I was in China being treated for cancer. Although I had surgery for an ovarian tumor in San Francisco, I was left with microscopic cancer cells in the peritoneal cavity, and needed additional treatment. As a practicing acupuncturist, I knew that herbs would help build my immune system while I was on chemotherapy. However, in 1980 this option wasn't available to me in the United States, but I was very fortunate to be invited to China to receive this combined therapy.

The hospitals in China had both Western medicine and traditional Chinese medicine available for patients. I thought that this was a wonderful model for the United States, and from this idea, the concept for the International Health Center was created. Our vision for the International Health center is to bring Eastern and Western medicine under one roof, and expand the health-care options for the consumer.

While I was in China, I learned how the Chinese deal

with problems of illness, not only cancer. As a matter of fact, when I was first met at the airport by the Assistant Director of Public Health in Shanghai, we were sharing with each other how we treat patients in the United States and also in China. The thing that impressed me so much was, she said that in China, patients get 70 percent care and 30 percent medication. That made a great impression upon me. This is the human quality of care that we want to bring into the International Health Center.

ANDREW: You know, Barbara, this is my whole direction as well. I talk about "integrative medicine." I would like to see physicians trained in being able to combine the best ideas and practices of conventional medicine and alternative medicine. It's not always using one in place of the other; it's knowing when and when not to use standard allopathic medicine, when and when not to use these other systems. All these systems have aspects that are sensible and some that aren't, and it's a matter of sorting the wheat from the chaff, and then building new combinations of all that's available out there.

SANDRA McLANAHAN: It's very exciting to see how quickly these changes are being embraced by Western medicine, that ultimately what really matters is what works. There's a great phrase from Winston Churchill: "I trust America to do the right thing, after having exhausted all other options." So I think in the West, we've exhausted a lot of options about how to feel good. And we're ready to look at some of these ancient traditions with new eyes.

In fact, these very simple but very profound practices can enrich the quality of our lives.

Most people who come to see me have tried all different options and are ready to try something new. They're in pain, and suffering. I think we see this as a result of the kind of out-of-balance lifestyle that we in the West have gotten caught up in. We're just very much outputting more than we're inputting as a culture. I think we have many elements of toxic culture right now.

So I think what we're going to have to do to get social support, which is very important to individual health as well as to our society's health, is to create a new kind of global family. Maybe something like intimacy circles, because I think that lifestyle changes are most successful with group support. If you don't have that, it's very difficult to maintain the changes in diet and exercise and relaxation that are necessary to maintain health.

So [let's have] intimacy circles of some sort—and they can be sort of flexible. And for those of us who travel a lot, as I do, they can be including every person that you meet, and then we can really get a sense that we have a global family happening. I think that's really fundamental to the health of our planet, because we're very social creatures, humans, and if we don't have a good social support, we tend to then act in ways that are either self-destructive or destructive to the larger whole.

These things are all important to a larger definition of medicine, too. I don't think that we can any longer define *medicine* as simply *individual health.* When I went to medical school, in the late 1960s, early 1970s, medical school was just drugs-and-surgery school, and that's what it still is in most places. That's all that is being taught, and those are the only tools. But it is changing, and I feel really encouraged that it will change. And all the different traditions from around the world will be incorporated to help us have a larger definition of medicine that includes the societal origins of illness, the need for social connection as part of the mind/body connection.

BARBARA: Today in America we are a multicultured society. However, we only offer Western medicine to all of these multicultural peoples. A few years ago, I met a professor, Herman Blake, who did research on how the black Americans in Tennessee were wanting their own kind of medicine. Even though for generations, they lived in America and their forefathers were Americans, they still wanted to go back and have African-type medicine. So we need to offer more types of medicine for the multicultural society.

ROBERT DUGGAN: When somebody comes into the clinic here, I will say to them, "Now, I want you to tell me about all the small symptoms, the things you'd never tell a doctor, and I assume that all of these symptoms are messengers. We want to learn how to understand the messengers and have them teach us how to get along well day to day." I will give them the example of somebody who once said to me, "I never thought asthma would become my friend." And I said, "What do you mean?" He said, "Well, when I came in, I was on a lot of prednisone, I was in and out of the hospital with severe asthmatic attacks. After treatment for two, three months, now I only get minor asthmatic symptoms. But when I get them, I know that I'm not paying attention to my diet, I'm having a fight with my wife, I'm not exercising, I'm working too much, and it becomes a reminder."

So what I think the theory of disease is, is that the body, mind, spirit are a whole, and that the symptoms that we get are ways, on the one hand, of protecting us, and on the other hand, of teaching us. I often use in speaking, the example of an elderly person with arthritic knees. Are the arthritic knees a problem that somebody should fix, or are the arthritic knees the wisdom slowing the person down so that he doesn't overstretch his heart or his inner energy? And that is a place where I think we have a totally different philosophy. I don't see anybody around who doesn't cope with suffering and death, and the philosophy out of which I've studied and worked is that life is about dancing with pain and suffering and death, rather than trying to prevent suffering and death.

There is the role of someone who devotes themselves to being present to others in their pain, to hold them in their pain, not to be afraid of their pain, and knowing ways that they themselves or that others have to keep the pain moving. The Chinese philosophy about life includes the image of the lid on the rice pot going up and down with the steam coming up out of it, and that's the picture of life moving, the steam coming up, and the lid going up and down. So the role of the healer is the one who can keep the steam on the pot at the right temperature so it keeps bouncing up and down, and life keeps moving rather than getting stuck. When it's stuck, you have disease. I think it's the art of being present to each person uniquely, and the healers are those who are willing to expand their own range of being in life sufficiently that they can be with more and more people comfortably, reflecting both the joys and the pain of life.

BARBARA: I think that what Robert Duggan was referring to as being the healer is possible for each one of us—to be our own healer, and to discover what it is within us that will make the changes necessary to keep ourselves healthy, and also overcome disease if we are sick.

ANDREW: My present interest and the subject of my writing is the healing system of the body. I'm fascinated by the fact that I never learned anything about that in medical school. You know, I learned about a circulatory system, the digestive system, the endocrine system. I never heard about a healing system. It's obvious that there is one. Why don't we hear about it? I think there are two reasons. One is that the healing system is not a structural system like those other systems. I can't hang up a wall chart of it. It's a functional system. Western medicine is not very well adapted to looking at functional systems. It deals with form and structure. Chinese medicine is much more focused on function. And another reason is that the whole focus in the training of physicians has been, as I said earlier, on disease, rather than on health and on healing. It's astonishing that we have done no research on the phenomenon of remission. Why isn't there a year's course in medical school on remission to balance the course in pathology? You know, the emphasis is very lopsided. So again, all this points to the need for new paradigms, new institutions, new ways of training practitioners, fundamental change, not tinkering with the mechanics of reimbursement.

VASANT LAD: The Ayurvedic approach is rather preventive, while modern medicine—if there is any problem directly—they give antihistamines or steroids or antibiotics to control the infection. It works only in acute conditions, and it is very effective medicine for suppressing the further properties of the disease. So the difference between modern medicine and Ayurveda is that Ayurveda gives us radical change, a change of lifestyle. Ayurveda is not a quick fix. It takes time. On the other hand, modern medicine apparently looks like a quick fix, but it is a suppression therapy. If a person has asthma, they give bronchodilators and steroids, and that suppresses the asthma, and people live with asthma throughout their lives. But the Ayurvedic approach to that is to eliminate the mucus from the system by doing *panchakarma*, which is a cleansing program, detoxification program, so that one can completely eradicate the pathogenesis of asthma. So Ayurvedic approach is slow, steady but perfect, and modern medicine approach is quick fix and suppression therapy.

The deeper cause of the illness is the imbalance of bodily *dosha*, and they say the deeper cause of the disease is bacteria, the virus, the antigen. So Ayurveda says that we are always living in the bacteria and virus and antigen; why and how can we improve our immune system? The Ayurvedic approach is to train the bodily cells to fight against the cause, like bacteria, viruses, and antigens. They enter the body, allergens; they enter the body and they start aggravating the symptoms.

That's why I think the approach of Ayurveda is very, very radical, basic and fundamental to eliminate those toxicities from the tissue so that tissue will be trained to fight against the infection and the person can develop the immunity. But if a person has low immunity, he needs antibiotics and steroids and antihistamines. It is okay to use, just in an emergency, so modern medicine has a right place in treating the emergencies, and Ayurveda has a right place in treating in [both a] preventive and curative way.

MICHAEL: *One of the terms used frequently in Ayurveda, which you just mentioned, is* dosha. *Can you define what* dosha *is?*

VASANT: Dosha is bodily humors, like *vata, pitta, kapha*. They make up internal bodily organization. They are responsible for psychobiological and psychopathological changes in the body. They are the energies.

Every disease has a definite structure. Which dosha—vata, pitta, kapha—is out of balance? Which tissues are affected? Which *dhatus*, that is, tissues, are involved, and which organs are suffering? Then there are specific herbs acting on those tissues, organs, and systems, and there are specific herbs and cleansing programs for respective bodily humors so that we can eradicate the complex network of the disease. So, Ayurveda doesn't treat the label like "cancer" or "AIDS" or "Epstein-Barr virus" or "Chronic

Fatigue Syndrome." But Ayurvedic recognizes that something is definitely happening in the body, and [what] is happening is connected with which dosha is out of balance, which tissues are affected, which organ is involved, and then Ayurveda does rejuvenation of the tissues, revitalization of the organs, and detoxification of the bodily doshas, so that the person can eradicate the problem. So the Ayurvedic approach is rather basic and fundamental.

Ayurveda says that every cell is a center of awareness, and the flow of awareness from one cell to another is called "intelligence." And that flow of intelligence is called *prana*. And there are different types, such as *prana vata*. For example, if the prana vata, which is responsible for movement, is stuck into certain tissues, then the prana doesn't move, the chi doesn't flow. Then that tissue works under stress, and the immunity of that tissue gets affected, then that tissue becomes susceptible to the repeated infection. That is what dosha is. Dosha is a flow of energy.

ANDREW: Ayurvedic medicine has not been very familiar to the West until recently. It's largely unresearched by Western medicine. There's a vast herbal pharmacopoeia. In fact, the herbal pharmacopoeia of India probably even surpasses that of China because India is a subtropical-tropical area. There's a much greater diversity of flora there. There is a great deal of Western interest currently in the Chinese pharmacopoeia, and there have been many instances in which, by the methods of Western science, we've been able to verify the traditional indications of many of the plants that have been used for centuries in

China. It would be useful to see some of that attention turned to this vast wealth of Indian plants that has been used for so long in Ayurvedic medicine.

BARBARA: It would be interesting to make a comparison of many other cultures that use herbs—the Native Americans, South Americans, and those that live in the Amazon rainforest. I was struck by several things that Vasant Lad said. Of course Ayurvedic medicine theory is very similar to the theory of Chinese medicine, where we deal also with the energy system. However, there are methods of prevention that [people] can use by themselves, and we have forms of practice that we call *qi gong* [pronounced *chee gong*]. Qi gong is the most ancient form of practice of the Chinese. The breathing, meditative exercises, and all the martial arts come from that practice. Aikido, kung fu, tai chi chuan, which are used for defense, and then there are those that are used for prevention, and each person can learn how to use them to keep [him- or herself] healthy.

◈ ◈ ◈

SUMMARY

Chinese, Tibetan, and Ayurvedic medicines focus on bringing the body into balance, strengthening the immune system, and preventing disease. Western doctors are not well trained in prevention techniques. Bob Duggan told us about a very fine doctor who said, "I am trained, and well trained, with what to do if somebody has an ulcer. The day before it's an ulcer, nobody's taught me what to do with it. I don't know anything about that." Western doctors are quite skillful, however, at treating emergencies and dealing with acute care. The development of antibiotics and other acute-care treatments has been a specialty of Western medicine. An integrated approach that makes use of the strengths of each type of medical practice can give patients the most effective care possible. If a person has an acute illness, it can be brought under control with Western practices; then, after the acute stage has passed, Asian medicine can help strengthen the body's systems to rid the body of the disease and prevent a recurrence.

◈◈◈◈◈

CHAPTER NINE

The Impact of Diet, Nutrition, and Touch on the Healing Process

Contributors:

Marian Williams, R.N., C.M.T., is Massage Therapy Program Coordinator at California Pacific Medical Center, where she established the Massage Therapy Internship program in 1990. This program brings hands-on experience to massage interns, and healing-touch therapy to inpatients in a hospital setting.

John McDougall, M.D., is a specialist on health and diet; Director of the McDougall Program at St. Helena Hospital in St. Helena, California; and the bestselling author of *The McDougall Plan* and *Twelve Days to Dynamic Health.*

Andrew Weil, M.D. (see bio on page 1)
Barbara Bernie, C.A. (see bio on page 75)
Harriet Beinfield, L.Ac. (see bio on page 33)

◈ ◈ ◈

MICHAEL TOMS: First, let's talk a little about diet and nutrition, and then go into the benefits of touch during the healing process.

HARRIET BEINFIELD: If someone has skin eruptions, volcanic heat that's erupting from the skin in the form of acne, then that kind of condition is going to be aggravated by them eating hot, spicy food. If somebody is internally cold and is living on a diet of raw salad and fruit, this is going to aggravate their condition. So in Chinese thinking, there aren't good foods and bad foods. The type of food you eat should be matched to the type of person you are. If you've got too much internal heat, you need to eat cooling foods. If you've got too much internal cold, you want to be drinking ginger tea and eating cooked foods. So what we've tried to do in teaching people about Chinese medicine is to help them figure out who they are so they can match their diet to their personal profile. The contribution that Chinese medicine has, I think, is in not making blanket judgments—milk doesn't do all bodies good. Animal protein is good for some people, in certain quantities, in certain forms and not for others. The real contribution of Chinese medicine is matching whatever it is, whether it's a medicine or a food, to the constitution of the person who is going to be making use of it.

JOHN McDOUGALL: The number-one cause of food allergy is dairy. I mean, that's so far ahead of anything else that when you start looking for other problems, you have to go way down the line. Eggs are close to dairy, also, but generally, just by following a starch-based meal plan, you've solved most of the allergy problems because you've eliminated the dairy products and the egg products. Now, for some people, that's not satisfactory. I'd say you're looking at a small percentage, maybe five, ten percent of the people who follow a healthy diet have to go further. Wheat would be next, and then corn and then citrus; of course, nuts bother a lot of people. They'd be even above wheat. Sometimes people have to do something called an "elimination program." That consists of foods that you are least likely to be allergic to, like brown rice and sweet potatoes and green and yellow vegetables thoroughly cooked, and no citrus fruits. It's a tough diet, but it is a good tool. You can figure out so many problems—rashes, arthritis problems, intestinal sensitivities, asthma problems, and others.

***MICHAEL:** Can you explain more about the "elimination diet"?*

JOHN: First you pick the foods that you're least likely to be allergic to—you could be allergic to brown rice, but it's very, very, very rare. You eat this diet for a week, and it takes about four or five days to clean the system out of the other foods. You get well. If you don't get well, it's not a dietary problem. But assuming you're going to get well, which does happen in most cases, then what you do is you start adding foods back, and see which ones make you sick, what gives you the headaches, the arthritis, and so on. So you add large amounts back of, say, wheat. After two days of eating wheat, if your headaches return or your arthritis gets worse, or your rash flares up, then you know you've got a problem with wheat, and you eliminate it from the diet. So what you do is an investigation, which is not popular, because it takes work.

You know, everyone wants to lay back and say, "Fix me, give me allergy tests, give me pills, give me shots." This program is simple and it's free, it doesn't cost anything. You can't charge people for it. So it's not very popular with the medical business, because of course we want to do things to you so we can feel powerful and we can also make money at it. But it is the standard. In other words, the standard treatment and the standard test for allergy is to eliminate what's making you sick, and you get well. And then to add it back in and to confirm that it was the problem. So everything—any test, any treatment—has to be referenced against elimination of the substance. And so you might as well go to the direct source by following the elimination diet, the ultimate in giving you relief.

ANDREW: I say it's possible to put too much emphasis on diet and to see it as the sole cause of disease and the only factor of importance in health. I always ask patients to make changes in how they eat, but I do that because I think that for people to change the way they eat, that represents a big commitment of mental energy in the direction of healing. People are very fixed in their ways of eating. If you can motivate a person to make a change in eating in order to improve their health, it represents a major shift. I think that kind of shift might activate internal healing mechanisms so that dietary changes may have healing power far out of proportion to the content of the changes. I think it's important to recognize that dimension of eating and diet as factors in health.

BARBARA: I would go along with that, too, and I would like to expand further on what Harriet had to say, because in Chinese medicine we do have another method of diagnosing, which is called the *differential diagnosis.* We talk about food being hot, wet, cold, dry, and yin/yang imbalances, et cetera. We also talk about disease as being a hot disease, a cold disease, a wet/dry imbalance of yin/yang, et cetera, so that depending upon what your diagnosis is—and it changes all the time—we would recommend specific foods. For example, if a person comes in and we know that person has cancer, we consider cancer a hot disease. We would not recommend certain things such as shellfish, which is considered toxic and hot, coffee, any alcohol or drink of that type, chocolate, and various other foods that are considered hot.

ANDREW: I think all this has to be said against the background of almost total neglect of nutrition in Western medicine and medical training. I have often said that in my four years at Harvard Medical School and a year of internship, the total instruction I got in nutrition was 30 minutes. That 30 minutes was grudgingly allowed to a dietitian at one hospital I worked at in Boston to tell us about special diets we could order for patients. This situation has not changed a whole lot since I've been out of medical school. I think that this defect in medical education is the one that the general public is most aware of. There are many other defects, but that one, I think, the public has become aware of.

Look at the food served in hospitals. The largest hospital in Phoenix some years ago opened a McDonald's restaurant in the hospital, as the hospital restaurant. This is now a trend around the country. The hospital sees this as a good thing. It's a draw to the hospital. They don't see any problem there.

Several years ago, my father, who was then 77, had emergency coronary bypass surgery at a leading hospital in Philadelphia. I was summoned back there. I was told he might not live through the operation. On the plane back, I just made a mental decision that I was not going to be involved in this; I'd be emotionally detached, let them do whatever they wanted. I lost it almost immediately when I got there and saw the first meal sent up to him after he came back from surgery. It was a pastrami sandwich and vanilla ice cream.

I got on the phone with the hospital dietitian, and she could not understand why I was upset. She said they were trying to stimulate his appetite. She saw no incongruity there. So we've got a lot of problems to overcome in dealing with our diets.

MICHAEL: *Let's talk a little about the effects of touch on the healing process.*

MARIAN WILLIAMS: A massage therapist told me about going into a unit, and one of the nursing staff said, "Oh, are you the massage therapist coming on again today? I checked with all my patients last night, and all three of the patients who had received a massage—none of them required a sleeping pill that night—whereas normally they require a sleeping pill every night." Another example is when you're working with a patient who may be experiencing a lot of pain, and may be curled up almost in a fetal position. You go in with a presence and a calm and provide touch to them in a caring, nurturing, compassionate way, and they begin to melt, unwind, and breathe more deeply, and some oftentimes fall into a deep sleep that they may have been deprived of up until that point.

I hear stories over and over again from patients who have received massage, who talk about how important it is for them. They say it seems to free up their own energies so that they can focus on their own healing. The nurses report that they feel that massage really helps to facilitate the human process for their patients. They say they love the service because they feel like it makes their job easier. It's something that they can offer their patients, oftentimes when they have no other recourse or there may be no other medications to offer them for anxiety or pain or restlessness. This is a very noninvasive, caring way to provide relaxation and comfort to patients, to help that healing process and really to serve as an adjunct to the current medical regime.

I remember working with one patient who had received numerous back surgeries. I'd received a call to go, and I went to see her. She was planning on returning home within a couple days. Oftentimes we may not receive any feedback when we're working with patients directly, particularly if they go to sleep afterwards, unless we check with them later, or hear it from the nursing staff. She said that when she came into the hospital, she felt that she had to give her body over to the doctors. She'd had her surgery, and there was little control over a lot of things that she had to go through. Then, by getting the massage, she felt like that was her way of reclaiming her body herself. She felt that it really put her on the road to recovery and made her feel that when she went home, she could again have control. That is very empowering for the patient.

ANDREW: I think it's great. I think it's very great for the person who does the massage and the person who receives it. I had no experience with massage in my medical training. A few years after I'd finished my clinical training, I discovered the wonderful world of massage and became very excited about its therapeutic potentials. I remember looking on my bookshelf for a manual for clinical practitioners, which was very comprehensive of all therapies. I looked up *massage*, and there was an entry in the index for [that term]. Very excitedly, I turned to that page, and on that page there was a list. The word *massage* was the last word in the list, and the list was headed "Methods of Psychological Value Only." I think that says so much about the orientation of thinking of the past.

Even if it were of psychological value only, that would be great, but it's not of psychological value only. I send a lot of patients to different kinds of body therapies. There are great traditions of using massage therapeutically, especially in Oriental medicine where there are some very highly developed forms of pressure massage. Even on a very mundane level, I have seen cases of tension headache that had consumed vast sums of money in fruitless attempts to diagnose them or to treat them that were solved by having patients get, on a regular basis, neck and shoulder massages, especially at the end of a workday.

BARBARA: I remember, during one trip in China, I was taken to a clinic where they do special massage, which is called *tui na,* a therapeutic massage. A little baby was brought there, a six-month-old baby who was suffering with diarrhea, uncontrollable diarrhea. The Western medical physicians couldn't help this child, so they brought it to this tui na clinic. The baby was six months old, and the practitioner was kneading the body as you would dough. The baby was gurgling and loving every bit of it, and more importantly, the baby was getting well.

MICHAEL: *So, is there a time that you see coming where we'll have this kind of therapy in the hospital, or in the health center? It's a natural component of the healing process.*

BARBARA: Actually, we use it in our clinic. We use all these methods of health care right in our clinic whenever it's needed.

ANDREW: At the European health spas, especially in German-speaking locations, they have long traditions at places where there are mineral waters with therapeutic value. Massage is a very important component of these therapies, and often government insurance will reimburse for patients to go to these spas. I think there are models that are out there that we can look at, that can help us design our health and healing centers.

◈ ◈ ◈

SUMMARY

Nutrition:

What we put in our mouth provides the materials for our bodies to live and grow and be healthy. Each of the cells in our body changes over time, so the body you have right now is not the same one you had last year. Yet many doctors have no knowledge of how their patients' diets affect their health because they weren't taught about nutrition in medical school. Now, however, more attention is being paid to nutrition. Some doctors have shown that changing to a low-fat vegetarian diet, along with other lifestyle changes, can reverse the build-up of plaque in coronary arteries. Eastern medical practices indicate that including or deleting particular foods in one's diet can promote healing and strengthen the immune system. Specific foods recommended are determined by the body type of the individual, the energy system in the body that needs balancing, and the qualities of the food itself. For example, according to Chinese medical theory, if you have too much internal cold, you should balance it by drinking ginger tea and eating more cooked foods. Teenagers can reduce acne by avoiding hot spicy foods that aggravate such "heat" conditions. Some people claim to have been cured of cancer by eating a macrobiotic diet. USDA botanist James Duke has been researching the preventive and healing properties of foods we eat every day. As more scientific proof mounts about the use of foods to promote health, we expect that our medical schools will begin to educate doctors in this area.

Touch:

We often take our bodies for granted until an illness or injury calls our attention to a part that is not working. Most of us were not encouraged to listen to our body as we grew up, so we may ignore signals that could help us prevent full-blown illnesses. While we may have heard that exercise or massage is good for us, we often feel too busy to find time for it. Over the past 20 years, there has been a growing wealth of information on ways to help our bodies stay healthy through movement and massage. Much of this information comes from Eastern healing traditions. Yoga, t'ai chi, qi gong, aikido, and many other practices help the body to balance and rejuvenate when practiced regularly.

There are many types of massage therapy that have been developed to relax and realign our bodies. These range from Swedish massage to Trager bodywork, tui na, shiatsu, and the deep tissue work of Rolfing. A cancer patient in China developed a very simple form of qi gong that is now widely used by cancer patients there. The movements in these practices are a way of providing an internal massage to yourself when you don't have time for a massage.

Massage has been shown to be particularly effective in hospitals to help patients relax prior to surgery, reduce the amount of pain medication needed, allow patients to sleep without sleeping pills, and to give them a sense of reowning their body after surgery. The use of massage and movement can help us be in touch with what is happening in our bodies, and to bring them back to balance and health.

◈◈◈◈◈

Discussion Questions

PART I

CHAPTER 1: THE CHANGING DYNAMICS IN THE DOCTOR/PATIENT RELATIONSHIP

- Give examples of how communication between you and your doctor affects your health.
- Discuss some specific ways in which you take responsibility for your own health care.
- Have you seen or experienced a case of psychological malpractice or "doctor hexing"? How would you deal with a situation like that to neutralize its effect on your health?
- Do you feel you can trust your own inner wisdom about health or healing? Give an example of a time when you used it.

CHAPTER 2: PATIENT-CENTERED CARE—CREATING A NEW PARADIGM IN MIND/BODY MEDICINE

- If you or a loved one has had a recent hospital experience, were there any aspects of it that you would consider patient-centered care? Explain.
- Have you ever done research seeking information about an illness? How were you affected by educating yourself about that illness?
- What do you see as the advantages and disadvantages of patient-centered care?

CHAPTER 3: QUESTIONS OF ETHICS

- Have you had the experience of needing to make an ethical choice in health care, including giving or withholding care from someone? Discuss your experience. If you have not had that experience, what choices do you think you would make and why?
- When do you think life support should be removed? What are the most important considerations in making that decision?
- What would you want to include in a living will or other document to make sure your care follows your wishes if you are too ill to express them?

CHAPTER 4: BELIEF SYSTEMS AND HEALTH

- What specific beliefs do you see influencing the choices you make in daily living that affect your health?
- In addition to your belief system, what other factors influence your health-care choices?
- How have your beliefs about health and medicine been influenced by your personal experiences with mainstream medicine or complementary therapies?
- How do you explain the occurrence of spontaneous remissions and "miraculous" cures?

PART II

CHAPTER 5: ALTERNATIVE THERAPIES FOR HEART DISEASE AND CANCER

- Discuss examples of ways in which you have seen emotions, values, lifestyle, and social support affect physical diseases.
- Describe a time in your life when you experienced first-hand the relationship between physical, psychological, and spiritual well-being.
- Do your doctors or other care givers take your psychological and spiritual state into account when they treat you? Explain. What could you do to encourage them?

- Discuss specific ways in which your dietary choices relate to your experience and understanding of health, illness, and healing.
- New medical uses are being found for plants on a regular basis. What does this say about the destruction of plant species through pollution and development, and the global implications of these practices?
- What are the implications for our health-care system of a limit to research into the preventative or healing properties of plants caused by the high costs of that research? What can be done to remedy this situation?

The Commonweal Cancer Help Program is about creating a space for healing and helping people to look at the choices they can make. Michael Lerner delineates five areas of choice that are important for everyone in the second half of life to explore, whether they have a life-threatening illness or not. These areas are: the choices you'd make in healing; the choices you'd make in mainstream medicine; the choices you'd make in complementary approaches; the choices you'd make in pain control; and the choices you'd make in dying.

By exploring each of these areas, you can learn what is possible and decide the approaches that fit with your life and what is important to you. You can develop skill, knowledge, choice, and control in each area. The questions in this book, and the resources listed here, can help you to begin your exploration. Lerner says to those with life-threatening diseases: Whether or not you can change the direction of your disease, you can transform it, and there are things to know in each of these areas that can be profoundly useful to you. Take some time to begin a journal that you can use to chart your exploration.

CHAPTER 6: THE RELATIONSHIP BETWEEN ATTITUDE, SPIRITUALITY, AND HOMEOPATHY

- What do you see as some of the ramifications of questioning—or not questioning—your doctor's orders? How comfortable do you feel asking these questions?
- If something felt wrong about care that you were about to be given, how would you respond?
- In your view, what is the relationship of optimism, anger, or other emotions to healing?
- Give an example of how you have participated in your own care during an illness. In what way do you think this affected the course of your illness?

PART III

CHAPTER 7: COMPLEMENTARY MEDICINE: TODAY AND TOMORROW

- Have you ever used any form of complementary therapy? If yes, why did you choose to use this therapy? Describe your specific experiences.

- In your view, what are the advantages and disadvantages of complementary therapies?
- How has your personal perception and understanding of complementary therapies changed in the last few years?
- How can complementary therapies best be integrated with mainstream medicine in a comprehensive health-care system?

CHAPTER 8: NEW APPROACHES TO HEALTH CARE: A DISCUSSION

- How have your perceptions of such therapies as acupuncture, yoga, and shiatsu massage changed over the past five years? What do you think accounts for their increasing availability and use?
- What do you see as the advantages or disadvantages of Asian therapies?
- Have you used Asian and Western medicines to complement each other? Explain.
- How does the use of complementary medicine, such as herbs or acupuncture, fit in with your own beliefs and values?

CHAPTER 9: THE IMPACT OF DIET, NUTRITION, AND TOUCH ON THE HEALING PROCESS

Nutrition:

- In what specific ways have you experienced a relationship between the foods you eat and your health?
- What family, ethnic, or cultural traditions about food, eating, and so on did you learn earlier in life, and how have these affected your health?
- Have you ever been told to eat or avoid certain foods for your health? If so, did you follow the advice? What was the outcome?
- Describe some of the ways in which cultural attitudes about food, as expressed in the media, shape our dietary habits and influence health.

Touch:

- Describe your experience of health and illness in physical terms.
- In what specific ways do you pay attention to signals from your body related to health or illness?
- Why do you think movement practices and massage have become so popular?
- How has your use of massage or your practice of movement affected your experience of yourself, your body, your health, or your capacity for healing?

Self-Help Resources

The following list of resources can be used for more information about recovery options for issues surrounding addictions, health concerns, death and bereavement, or problems related to dysfunctional families. The addresses and telephone numbers listed are for the national headquarters; look in your local yellow pages under "Community Services" for resources closer to your area.

In addition to the following groups, other self-help organizations may be available in your area to assist your healing and recovery for a particular life crisis not listed here. Consult your telephone directory, call a counseling center or help line near you, or contact:

American Self-Help Clearinghouse
St. Clares-Riverside Medical Center
Denville, NJ 07834
(201) 625-7101

National Self-Help Clearinghouse
25 West 43rd St., Room 620
New York, NY 10036
(212) 642-2944

AIDS

AIDS Hotline
(800) 342-2437

Children with AIDS Project of America
4020 N. 20th St., Ste. 101
Phoenix, AZ 85016
(602) 265-4859
Hotline:
(602) 843-8654

The Names Project - AIDS Quilt
(800) 872-6263

National AIDS Network
(800) 342-2437

Project Inform
19655 Market St., Ste. 220
San Francisco, CA 94103
(415) 558-8669

PWA Coalition
50 W. 17th St.
New York, NY 10011

Spanish AIDS Hotline
(800) 344-7432

TDD (Hearing Impaired) AIDS Hotline
(800) 243-7889

◈◈◈

ALCOHOL ABUSE

Al-Anon Family Headquarters
200 Park Ave. South
New York, NY 10003
(804) 563-1600

Alcoholics Anonymous (AA)
General Service Office
475 Riverside Dr.
New York, NY 10115
(212) 870-3400

Children of Alcoholics Foundation
P.O. Box 4185
Grand Central Station
New York, NY 10163-4185
(212) 754-0656
(800) 359-COAF

Meridian Council, Inc.
Administrative Offices
4 Elmcrest Terrace
Norwalk, CT 06850

National Association of Children of Alcoholics (NACOA)
11426 Rockville Pike, Ste. 100
Rockville, MD 20852
(301) 468-0985

National Clearinghouse for Alcohol and Drug Information (NCADI)
P.O. Box 234
Rockville, MD 20852
(301) 468-2600

National Council on Alcoholism and Drug Dependency (NCADD)
12 West 21st St.
New York, NY 10010
(212) 206-6770

◈◈◈

ANOREXIA/BULIMIA

American Anorexia/Bulimia Association, Inc.
293 Central Park West, Ste. 1R
New York, NY 10024
(212) 501-8351

Eating Disorder Organization
1925 East Dublin Granville Rd.
Columbus, OH 43229-3517
(918) 481-4044

CANCER

National Cancer Institute
(800) 4-CANCER

ECAP (Exceptional Cancer Patients)
Bernie S. Siegel, M.D.
300 Plaza Middlesex
Middletown, CT 06457
(860) 343-5950

◈◈◈

CHILDREN'S ISSUES

Child Molestation

Adults Molested As Children United (AMACU)
232 East Gish Rd.
San Jose, CA 95112
(800) 422-4453

National Committee for Prevention of Child Abuse
332 South Michigan Ave., Ste. 1600
Chicago, IL 60604
(312) 663-3520

Children's and Teens' Crisis Intervention

Boy's Town Crisis Hotline
(800) 448-3000

Covenant House Hotline
(800) 999-9999

Kid Save
(800) 543-7283

National Runaway and Suicide Hotline
(800) 621-4000

◈◈◈

Missing Children

Missing Children-Help Center
410 Ware Blvd., Ste. 400
Tampa, FL 33619
(800) USA-KIDS

National Center for Missing and Exploited Children
1835 K St. NW
Washington, DC 20006
(800) 843-5678

Children with Serious Illnessees (fulfilling wishes)

Brass Ring Society
(918) 743-3232

◈◈◈

CO-DEPENDENCY

Co-Dependents Anonymous
60 E. Richards Way
Sparks, NV 89431
(602) 277-7991

◈◈◈

DEATH/GRIEVING/SUICIDE

Grief Recovery Helpline
(800) 445-4808

Grief Recovery Institute
8306 Wilshire Blvd., Ste. 21A
Beverly Hills, CA 90211
(213) 650-1234

Mothers Against Drunk Driving (MADD)
(817) 690-6233

National Hospice Organization (NHO)
1901 Moore St. #901
Arlington, VA 22209
(703) 243-5900

National Sudden Infant Death Syndrome
Two Metro Plaza, Ste. 205
Landover, MD 20785
(800) 221-SIDS

Seasons: Suicide Bereavement
4777 Naniola Dr.
Salt Lake City, UT 84117

◈◈◈

DEBTS

Debtors Anonymous
General Service Office
P.O. Box 400
Grand Central Station
New York, NY 10163-0400
(212) 642-8220

DIABETES

American Diabetes Association
(800) 232-3472

◈◈◈

DRUG ABUSE

Cocaine Anonymous
(800) 347-8998

National Cocaine-Abuse Hotline
(800) 262-2463
(800) COCAINE

National Institute of Drug Abuse (NIDA)
Parklawn Building
5600 Fishers Lane, Room 10A-39
Rockville, MD 20852
(301) 443-6245 (for information)
(800) 662-4357 (for help)

World Service Office (CA)
3740 Overland Ave. Suite C
Los Angeles, CA 90034-6337
(310) 559-5833

EATING DISORDERS

Eating Disorder Organization
1925 East Dublin Granville Rd.
Columbus, OH 43229-3517
(918) 481-4044

Overeaters Anonymous
National Office
Rio Rancho, NM
(505) 891-2664

◈◈◈

GAMBLING

Gamblers Anonymous
National Council on Compulsive Gambling
444 West 59th St., Room 1521
New York, NY 10019
(212) 903-4400

◈◈◈

HEALTH ISSUES

Alzheimer's Disease Information
(800) 621-0379

American Chronic Pain Association
P.O. Box 850
Rocklin, CA 95677
(916) 632-0922

American Foundation of Traditional Chinese Medicine
1280 Columbus Ave., Ste. 302
San Francisco, CA 94133
(415) 776-0502

American Holistic Health Association
P.O. Box 17400
Anaheim, CA 92817
(714) 779-6152

Chopra Center for Well-Being
Deepak Chopra, M.D.
7630 Fay Ave.
La Jolla, CA 92037
(619) 551-7788

The Fetzer Institute
9292 West KL Ave.
Kalamazoo, MI 49009
(616) 375-2000

Hippocrates Health Institute
1443 Palmdale Court
West Palm Beach, FL 33411
(407) 471-8876

Hospicelink
(800) 331-1620

Institute for Noetic Sciences
P.O. Box 909, Dept. M
Sausalito, CA 94966-0909
(800) 383-1394

The Mind-Body Medical Institute
185 Pilgrim Rd.
Boston, MA 02215
(617) 632-9525

National Health Information Center
P.O. Box 1133
Washington, DC 20013-1133
(800) 336-4797

Optimum Health Care Institute
6970 Central Ave.
Lemon Grove, CA 91945
(619) 464-3346

Preventive Medicine Research Institute
Dean Ornish, M.D.
900 Bridgeway, Ste. 2
Sausalito, CA 94965
(415) 332-2525

World Research Foundation
20501 Ventura Blvd., Ste. 100
Woodland Hills, CA 91364
(818) 999-5483

◈◈◈

IMPOTENCE

Impotency Institute of America
10400 Patuzent Pkwy, Ste. 485
Washington, DC 20006
(800) 669-1603

◈◈◈

INCEST

Incest Survivors Resource Network International, Inc.
P.O. Box 7375
Las Cruces, NM 88006-7375
(505) 521-4260

COURSE IN MIRACLES COUNSELORS

Miracle Distribution Center
1141 East Ash Ave.
Fullerton, CA 92631
(714) 738-8380
(800) 359-2246

◈◈◈

PET BEREAVEMENT

Bide-A-Wee Foundation
New York, NY
(212) 532-6395

The Animal Medical Center
510 E. 62nd St.
New York, NY 10021
(212) 838-8100

Holistic Animal Consulting Center
29 Lyman Ave.
Staten Island, NY 10305
(718) 720-5548

RAPE

Austin Rape Crisis Center
1824 East Oltorf
Austin, TX 78741
(512) 440-7273

◈◈◈

SEX ADDICTIONS

National Council on Sexual Addictions
P.O. Box 652
Azle, TX 76098-0652
(800) 321-2066

◈◈◈

SMOKING ABUSE

Nicotine Anonymous
2118 Greenwich St.
San Francisco, CA 94123
(415) 750-0328

SPOUSAL ABUSE

National Coalition Against Domestic Violence
P.O. Box 34103
Washington, DC 20043-4103
(202) 638-6388

National Domestic Violence Hotline
(800) 799-SAFE

◈◈◈

STRESS REDUCTION

The Biofeedback & Psychophysiology Clinic
The Menninger Clinic
P.O. Box 829
Topeka, KS 66601-0829
(913) 350-5000

New York Open Center
(In-depth workshops to invigorate the spirit)
83 Spring St.
New York, NY 10012
(212) 219-2527

Omega Institute
(A healing, spiritual retreat community)
260 Lake Dr.
Rhinebeck, NY 12572-3212
(914) 266-4444 (info)
(800) 944-1001 (to enroll)

Rise Institute
P.O. Box 2733
Petaluma, CA 94973
(707) 765-2758

The Stress Reduction Clinic
Jon Kabat-Zinn, Ph.D.
University of Massachusetts Medical Center
55 Lake Ave. North
Worcester, MA 01655
(508) 856-1616
(508) 856-2656

Recommended Reading

Ageless Body, Timeless Mind: The Quantum Alternative to Growing Old, by Deepak Chopra, M.D.

Between Heaven and Earth: A Guide to Chinese Medicine, by Harriet Beinfield and Efrem Korngold

Deep Healing: The Essence of Mind/Body Medicine, by Emmett E. Miller, M.D.

Dr. Dean Ornish's Program for Reversing Heart Disease, by Dean Ornish, M.D.

Full Catastrophe Living: Using the Wisdom of Your Body and Mind to Face Stress, Pain, and Illness, by Jon Kabat-Zinn, Ph.D.

Healing and the Mind, by Bill Moyers

Healing Journey, by O. Carl Simonton, M.D.

Healing the Heart, Healing the Body,
by Ron Scolastico, Ph.D.

Healing Words: The Power of Prayer and the Practice of Medicine,
by Larry Dossey, M.D.

Health and Healing, by Andrew Weil, M.D.

How to Live Between Office Visits,
by Bernie S. Siegel, M.D.

Mind/Body Medicine: How to Use Your Mind for Better Health,
by Daniel Goleman, Ph.D., and Joel Gurin

Kitchen Table Wisdom, by Rachel Naomi Remen, M.D.

The Power of the Mind to Heal,
by Joan Borysenko, Ph.D.,
and Miroslav Borysenko, Ph.D.

Quantum Healing: Exploring the Frontiers of Mind/Body Medicine, by Deepak Chopra, M.D.

Spontaneous Healing, by Andrew Weil, M.D.

Women's Bodies, Women's Wisdom,
by Christiane Northrup, M.D.

You Can Heal Your Life, by Louise L. Hay

NEW DIMENSIONS FOUNDATION

Since its inception in 1973, New Dimensions Foundation has presented lecture series, live events and seminars; published books, sponsored educational tours, and launched a major periodical. Created to address the dramatic cultural shifts and changing human values in our society, New Dimensions has become an international forum for some of the most innovative ideas expressed on the planet. Its principal and best-known activity is New Dimensions Radio, an independent producer of radio dialogues and other programming.

During the past 20 years, many of this century's leading thinkers and social innovators have spoken through New Dimensions. The programming supports a diversity of views from many traditions and cultures. Now is a time for transformative learning and for staying open to all possibilities. We must constantly be willing to review and revise what we are creating. New Dimensions fosters the goals of living a more healthy life of mind, body, and spirit while deepening our connections to self, family, community, environment, and planet.

New Dimensions is a rare entity in the world of media—a completely independent, noncommercial radio producer. Primary support comes from listeners. Members of "Friends of New Dimensions" (FOND) are active partners in a conspiracy of hope as we celebrate the human spirit and explore new ideas, provocative insights, and creative solutions across the globe over the airwaves.

You too can play an invaluable part in this positive force for change by becoming a member of (FOND) and supporting the continued production and international distribution of New Dimensions Radio programming.

Become a Member of FOND:

As a Member of "Friends of New Dimensions" (FOND), you will receive:

- *The New Dimensions Journal,* a bimonthly magazine containing captivating articles, reviews of books, video and audio tapes, current "New Dimensions" program schedules, selections of audio tapes from our archives, and much more.

- The New Dimensions Annual Tape Catalog and periodic supplements.

- A 15% discount on any product purchased through New Dimensions, including books, New Dimensions tapes, and selected tapes from other producers.

- A quality thank-you gift expressing our deepest appreciation.

- The satisfaction of knowing that you are supporting the broadcast of hopeful visions to people all across the nation and the world.

Contributions are tax deductible to the extent allowed by law.

A nonprofit tax-exempt educational organization
P.O. Box 569 • Ukiah, CA 95482 • 707-468-5215
Website: http://www.newdimensions.org
E-mail: ndradio@igc.org

◈◈◈◈◈

We hope you enjoyed this Hay House/New Dimensions book. If you would like to receive a free catalog featuring additional Hay House books and products, or if you would like information about the Hay Foundation, please contact:

Hay House, Inc.
P.O. Box 5100
Carlsbad, CA 92018-5100

(800) 654-5126
(800) 650-5115 (fax)

Please visit the Hay House Website at:
http://www.hayhouse.com
and the New Dimensions Website at:
http://www.newdimensions.org

◈◈◈◈◈